CHRISTIAN MARRIAGE

DEVOTIONALS FROM BOTH PERSPECTIVES

CHRISTIAN DEVOTIONAL COLLABORATIONS
BOOK SIX

DEVOTIONAL COLLABORATIONS   MICHAEL LACEY

DEBBY SIBERT   MIRANDA J. CHIVERS   BECKY SIMS

MIMI KROGER   ROBERT KAPEN   KATIE ARTHUR

JACKIE PERSEGHETTI   KRISTIAN KELLY

JACQUELINE POPE   DVORA ELISHEVA

SHERRI HOWARD

Edited by
JACKIE PERSEGHETTI
Edited by
MICHAEL LACEY

Devo Writers
COLLABORATIONS

ISBN (paperback): 978-1-954838-12-3

Cover design, formatting, production, and marketing by Michael Lacey with Story-Builds.com | DevoWriters.com | Michael@michaellacey.me
Story Builds Creative, 2680 Baptist Rd. Nesbit, MS 38651
This book contains affiliate links for Amazon purchases.

CONTENTS

Part II
OTHER FAITHFUL SPOUSES

FREE DEVOTIONALS AND STORIES

Want a copy of another Devo Writers Collaboration for free?!

Go to *read.ChristWriters.com*

Subscribe to get:

- Updates on future releases
- One free devotional ebook!
- author interviews and special offers
- invitations to participate (if you wish)
- free books and opportunities to win books and tablets

CALLING ALL WRITERS!

Are you a writer/author? Maybe you'd like to join the next collection! Check out Devo Writers Collaborations, or email Michael to see how to get involved.

DevoWriters.com

Also, be sure to check out the insiders' Facebook group to follow along and see how you can contribute:

facebook.com/groups/christiancollections

If you're an author and have any self-publishing needs like those used for this book (covers, formatting, production, marketing, Amazon Ads, book page optimization, best-seller strategies, etc.), contact Michael directly at:

michael@michaellacey.me.

SPECIAL THANKS

We always aim to donate half of the proceeds (after production costs) from each Devo Writers Collaboration to a related charity for the first year of each book release. Due to the high quality of these productions, it's rare that we've been able to give much, but we hope that changes as more people discover these books. You can help by sharing and reviewing them.

So, we collectively shout a big thank you for your "donation," and we have faith that you (and many others) will continue to draw nearer to God through these heartfelt writings.

ALSO, special thanks to Jackie Perseghetti for her brilliant editing of a large part of this book.

ONE MORE REQUEST!

The more reviews, the more readers we can attract, and the more people we can help. This is THE best way you can help: please leave an honest review* on Amazon!

Leaving a review on Amazon is simple and you don't need to read the entire book! Just read a few devos and then write a simple statement and/or rating about what you read. You can always edit your review later. And most importantly...

Thank you!

INTRODUCTION

I have had a difficult marriage, over 12 years in. There, I got that out of the way. One of my pet peeves is listening to or reading something from someone who seems to have everything figured out. When I see a 'happy' marriage or hear about how great a person's marriage is, I disconnect a bit. Either they are lying, or they've actually had a great, *seemingly* problem-free marriage. If that's the case, I'm happy for them; God gave them that gift and mutual wisdom so perhaps they could be more effective in other areas of their ministries.

However, that's a rare occurrence. We are all broken people with sharp, jagged edges who tend to hurt one another. The beauty of marriage is that God uses our mates to reveal areas in our hearts in need of His transforming power. I know that is true in my own marriage as God has used my wife to help grind down some of my sharp edges, and vice versa.

So, who would you rather take advice from:

1. Someone who's seemingly never had a problem in their marriage?
2. Someone who has stayed married for years—or decades—despite the difficulties?

You might think choice 1 is right because they must know the "secret." And it's possible they might, but they probably don't. They would likely have a hard time understanding the baggage and brokenness. Maybe they haven't had to learn how to confront their sin nature at the same level, learning to grow in resilience and wisdom while facing the flesh in themselves and their spouse. Maybe they've simply learned how to communicate properly. Sounds easy enough, right? Well, it hasn't been so easy for me!

This is why I invited these authors and friends to contribute to this book. They are "regular" folk pursuing Christ-centered marriages, and I can't wait for you to dig into their devotionals.

For over a year, I struggled with whether or not I should even write anything for the Christian Marriage devotional collaboration. And I am not alone. I had several people in this collection say they shouldn't or couldn't write for this, but I encouraged them to do it anyway.

Will every story resonate with your own? Perhaps not, but I know there will be at least one match among the thousands of readers we have. For those few stories that don't connect, you most likely know someone who is journeying through those similar circumstances for whom it does.

DISCLAIMER

The authors in this collaboration are from all over the world and have unique stories and varying viewpoints. Please note: the thoughts of one author do not represent the thoughts of all. If you have a concern or issue, please reach out to that author directly to seek clarity.

As with anything you read, hold it up to the Word of God to test it, and apply what the Holy Spirit leads you to apply.

Because every marriage can benefit from vulnerable, real-life encouragement, we hope the wisdom, teaching, and empathy in this book helps you and those with whom you share it. ***We know that Marriage is for good. It's God's idea, designed by Him and for Him.***

As you'll read in some of these writings, many of us don't feel qualified to share on this topic, but that's a lie from the enemy. ***Anyone who is chasing after God has a powerful story to tell, one that just might help break chains for the next reader of those words.*** Maybe it's time for you to share your own story. (See the "Calling All Writers!" page for more info.)

Godspeed,

-Michael Lacey, 7x Best-Selling Author and Devo Writer

PART I
DEVO WRITERS

Devo Writers Collaborations

Christian Marriage Authors

HAPPY OR HOLY?

MICHAEL LACEY

*"What if God designed marriage to make us holy more
than to make us happy?"*

— GARY THOMAS, *SACRED MARRIAGE*

Before I was married, one of my biggest pet peeves about marriage was how negatively married couples spoke. I would hear men talk about "the old ball-and-chain" and make people believe it was miserable being married. However, back then, I just thought they were damaging the institution and concept of marriage by bad-mouthing it. Over a decade of marriage has now helped me understand a little more about where that comes from and how easily statements can be misconstrued.

So, when I got married and started reading Gary Thomas's *Sacred Marriage*, I didn't even finish the first chapter. I misread the subtitle as "you can't be holy AND happy in marriage," and I felt the content was killing my honeymoon high. Now, I'm finally starting to understand the premise and even embrace it!

LET'S TAKE A QUICK PAUSE FOR A DISCLAIMER: DON'T GO READING THIS ONE ALOUD TO YOUR SPOUSE. THIS IS NOT THE KIND OF ADVICE OR PERSPECTIVE THAT WILL ENCOURAGE THEM. IT'S THE KIND YOU WRESTLE WITH PERSONALLY.

I've seen marriages end and new ones begin. Sometimes the next relationship seems better, but it often becomes a never-ending cycle of hurt—like watching the baggage claim conveyor revolve around and around, only to gather more baggage each time.

From watching people in the world, I've realized that I have a choice.

1. I can choose to be "happy" by ending a difficult marriage in search of a more "compatible" mate. It's a risk that will involve pain, but it might make me happier, if only for a while (though there are mixed studies on this).
2. I can choose to allow God to use my difficult situation and challenging spouse to sanctify me, to make me more holy. If I truly claim to be a Christ-follower, should that not be my aim?

"You are to be holy to me because I, the Lord, am holy, and I have set you apart from the nations to be mine."

— LEVITICUS 20:26 (CSB)

After reading through many passages on the topic, surely we should realize the value of sanctification—not only for our marriages but for every aspect of the Christ-centered life. Read for example, Romans 6:19 and 12:1-2, 1 Thessalonians 5:22-23, Leviticus 20:7-8, 26, and Hebrews 12:14-15.

I must allow Christ to change me, and that requires real work. There's more on this in the next devotional, and it all ties together. When facing your next marital struggle, consider these incredible teachings and promises from the word of God.

"And not only that, but we also boast in our afflictions, because we know that affliction produces endurance, endurance produces proven character, and proven character produces hope. This hope will not disappoint us, because God's love has been poured out in our hearts through the Holy Spirit who was given to us."

— ROMANS 5:3–5 (CSB)

"Consider it a great joy, my brothers and sisters, whenever you experience various trials, because you know that the testing of your faith produces endurance. And let endurance have its full effect, so that you may be mature and complete, lacking nothing."

— JAMES 1:2–4 (CSB)

God, allow these truths from Your word to take deep root in my life. Give me wisdom as I wrestle through the difficulties of marriage. Help me embrace the opportunity to know You more and better understand Your love for the church as I strive to better love my wife. And when it gets harder than hard, remind me that You love me enough to not leave me where I am. Show me the ways I can grow, serve, and love. In this, bring me the insight to joy that You've so secretly hidden in Your word._Thank You for revealing these truths to me.

WHO AM I?

MICHAEL LACEY

"Search me, God, and know my heart;
test me and know my concerns.
See if there is any offensive way in me;
lead me in the everlasting way."

— PSALM 139:23-24 (CSB)

If you follow my wife or me on social media, you may think we're the perfect family, with our three beautiful children, cute little house on a few acres, and a sweet guard dog named Lucy. We serve together at church on the worship team, work multiple jobs, and try (unsuccessfully) to manage more than we can handle. Nevertheless, as you may have read in the introduction to this book, I don't feel qualified to write on Christian marriage, despite being in a Christ-centered marriage for 12 years (and counting).

In case you are wondering if our so-called image is who we really are at all times... it's not. There's truth in there but not the whole truth. We have real struggles. Eleven years in, we finally responded to those struggles by seeking different types of counseling – both professional and with trusted leaders in our church. I'm learning that I have more personal problems than I thought.

Taking the spotlight off my wife and putting it on me has been a game-changer. Have you ever put a bright light on something you thought was clean? You end up seeing a lot more than you bargained for.

> "The process of building a better marriage requires working to become better individually as well as together."
>
> — TONY EVANS

What has helped us most is honestly taking quizzes to learn more about ourselves so we can each know what to work on, and better understand one another. A few of those great resources that are helping us are listed at the end of this devotional.

It's hard to see how much we each change over time, even some "non-negotiables" as we grow together and individually. Regardless of who we were or who we will be, I trust that God put us together, and we believe in the marriage covenant. I don't even allow "divorce" in my marriage dictionary.

I won't look for a way out when I can find a deeper way in, one that will surely be richer than any "new" or "different" thing can offer.

I do thank God that we share a belief system in Christianity. Some call this being "equally yoked." This means we go to the Bible and seek wise counsel to work things out in a Christ-like way...to which I clearly nail every time...ha!

One last caveat: while I'm working on myself, I must work hard to not grow more critical of my spouse. I'll leave you with this inspiring quote:

> "We found so much joy and peace when we began to celebrate who each other is, before complaining about who each other is not."

> — DESIRINGGOD.COM, "IS IT THE THOUGHT THAT COUNTS?"

Lord, help me to celebrate my wife and who she is rather than complain and wish she would change. Change me instead. Help me to understand who I am and who You've made me to be. Give me the wisdom, tools, counsel, and humility to work on myself. Renew my mind daily, guide me, and lead me as I lead my wife and family. Enable our children to see Your strength in our weaknesses, so they will seek You more than anything we can offer.

Additional Resources for growth:

- Emotional Intelligence 2.0
- Five Love Languages
- Taylor-Johnson Temperament Analysis
- 16personalities.com
- The Road Back to You (Enneagram Study)

ALL OVER AGAIN

MICHAEL LACEY

"For now we see in a mirror dimly, but then face to face. Now I know in part; then I shall know fully, even as I have been fully known."

— 1 CORINTHIANS 13:12 (ESV)

I recently listened to a book series about people who get reset to an early age after they die. One character was around fifty and happily married when he had to restart at eight years old. His one goal was to find his wife again. It made me wonder what I would do.

I would be more patient with Ashton. I would support her more in pursuing passions rather than her watching me chase my dreams, which only fed her resentment over years of marriage, *unbeknownst* to me. It should have been *"knownst!"*

The character in the book messed it up by waiting over ten years only to get in a rush. I so wish I could go back and treat her the way she needed. Now, over ten years into our marriage, I regret not being where we could have been. As romantic as it is to think about starting over, I know I can't fix the past. But I can keep working on it today. I can renew my mind and rebuild her trust in a man who wants good for her, not just wants her for good.

Just like this is ten+ years in the future of *past-Michael's* marriage, I can look ahead to see a stronger union. We'll always have regrets, but thoughts like this may help me have fewer.

How fitting that the Corinthian verse above ties into this concept yet follows the most powerful and iconic definition of love. And though it's speaking of more than just love between spouses, the first two attributes in 1 Corinthians 13:4 are the ones I wish I'd exhibited more: "love is patient and kind."

God, help me not to lose this insight You've so graciously dropped into me. I want to treat my wife better. I want to fix what I didn't do right in the first place. Help me to do that. Give me grace and wisdom when I fail, and lead me in Your ways. Amen.

PROVE IT

MICHAEL LACEY

"Do you love her?"... "Prove it."

$\mathcal{J}$ust after celebrating seven years of our marriage, we had one of our biggest fights. We had been planning to take a trip with my family over New Years. This trip with my dad, brothers, and our families meant a lot as it would be a time of processing the loss of my mother and our first Christmas/New Year season without her.

A day or two before we were to leave, my wife told me she and our son weren't going. When she backed out of the trip, it hurt in many ways. I was already raw and exposed, vulnerable and in need.

As crazy as it sounds, it gave me an insight to what it feels like for people heading towards separation or divorce. It also gave me a chance to grow and to choose to let it strengthen us rather than weaken us.

I often choose to feel everything and work it out in the moment while my wife chooses to be more to herself and process things alone. Maybe you could say she's rubber and

I'm glue, but that works the other way around as time goes on.

Sometimes we feel we should punish our spouse or give them the cold shoulder or rebuke them. Basically, if they don't feel the pain, they won't learn...right?

But that's not what God does. What has God's grace done for you? What if we poured grace out? What can it do for her?

So, in the sticky mess of hurts and pain, I began to give it to God. I imagined consulting godly men—better men than myself—who seemed to have been happily married for a long time.

The theoretical answers were similar. I took it to God and heard something I believe was from Him:

"Do you love her?"

I searched my heart, remembering my commitment at the altar and the times we've had, and replied, "Yes."

Then, I heard God say, *"Prove it."*

In addition to that, I felt a related inspiration.

"Surprise her."

Surprise! That became my word and my goal for the next few years.

My mind rang it with the phrase, *"Surprise everyone with grace."* I know men who rarely hear honest words from their families because they know how the man will respond. They walk on eggshells around this patriarch. I don't want that to be me.

What did Jesus often do? Without fail, he surprised people with His words and actions. They didn't always follow man's logic, which is what I usually try to use in my defense. So that is what I will do. I will strive to surprise. I will try to surprise her when she thinks she knows how I will respond. I will strive to prove that I love her.

. . .

Has it been perfect? Not even close. Is it the right perspective? Of course. I made a covenant with God to love this woman. Now, when I face frustration or disappointment, I remember the choice I made and continue to make. I hear God say, *"Do you love her?"*

Lord, help me to prove that I love my wife, not just to myself but to her. Help me surprise her with grace when she expects a harsh response. Help me to be like You as You always stand with open arms. Thank You, amen.

P.S. Just one day after that fight and revelation, I struggled with bringing it back up along with other things. A little insight into forgiveness:

If you have forgiven someone, or asked for it, then you need to release your right to bring it back up again. Consider God—He forgets it, sends it as far as East is from West. We can't forget without supernatural power and it takes supernatural power to choose not to remember.

Michael Lacey produces all of the Christian Devotional Collaborations, more info at DevoWriters.com.

CHRIST-FOLLOWER, HUSBAND,
FATHER OF 3, SINGER/SONGWRITER,
WORSHIP LEADER, WOODWORKER
7X BEST-SELLING AUTHOR

One thing most people remember about Michael is his prosthetic eye. A lawn dart accident claimed his left eye when he was 11. Not only has it given him a unique perspective on life, but it has deepened his trust in God and His sovereignty.

Now, Lacey writes and help others produce their own writings. Everyone has a story to tell, and Michael is equipped to help.

Coming from the rich musical and literary heritage of Mississippi, Michael writes fiction under M. Lacey, non-fiction as Michael Lacey, and writes soulful songs that honor God and real life.

(continued)

His non-fiction work comes from over a decade of leading worship and pastoring people, helping them encounter God and experience life change.

His degrees in math and english, vocational certificates, self-taught musicianship, and woodworking deepen his storytelling and ability to connect with anyone. And as a creator, Michael is always chasing passions and striving to be better.

On most days, you can find Michael with a mason jar of sweet tea or wrestling with his two young sons and beautiful baby girl. Through all these pursuits, Michael is building a life where he spends more time with his family while inspiring others to do the same.

Learn more (and get some free stuff) at michaellacey.me
instagram.com/michaellaceymusic
facebook.com/michael.l.lacey

THE BEST SOLUTION FOR ANY MARITAL DISCORD

DEBBY SIBERT

"You shall love the Lord your God with all your heart and with all your soul and with all your mind. This is the great and first commandment. And a second is like it: You shall love your neighbor as yourself."

— MATTHEW 22:37-39 (ESV)

It would be easy to blame our high rate of marital failure on things like not spending enough quality time together, allowing bitterness and resentment to build in our hearts and failing to keep communication lines open. While these are vitally important to creating a happy marriage, if such things aren't happening, it's usually a sign of a much deeper problem.

What I have experienced personally and as a result of working with struggling couples, is that at the root of all marital issues is a "heart" problem. Fix the heart, fix the marriage. What rules our heart shapes our relationships.

When we marry, we promise before God, family and friends to love and cherish one another until parted by death. How in the world do we do that? We can't in our own strength, but if the Lord is at the center of our lives, we have all we need to experience a thriving marriage.

How do we get there? We do so by getting our vertical relationship with the God of the Universe right wherein we experience Him intimately, and the Holy Spirit is active in our life, guiding and directing us into all truth. That is of paramount importance before any horizontal relationship has a chance of being all it can be. I have found that when I am feeling close to God, everything else seems to fall into place. At least I find myself more at peace, being able to rest in Him and more able to accept adversity as part of my life's journey, trusting Him to get me through it.

I believe that virtually every marital problem can be traced back to one or both spouses failing to abide by these two commandments. The minute we begin to focus on our own wants, needs, and expectations over those of God or our spouse, we're destined for a lack of harmony or unity. I have to admit that I definitely have a selfish bent. I like for things to go my way and that often guides my expectations. When my spouse has conflicting selfish expectations, you can see where that can lead.

Feeling bitterness and resentment growing toward your spouse? When was the last time you brought him or her before the Lord in prayer and truly thanked God for your relationship? Struggling to find quality time together? I have found that praying with my spouse and asking God how He would like us to use our time has often helped to restore intimacy.

I think you will find, as I have, that as you begin to do these things, you'll notice that your focus automatically starts to shift away from you, your desires and expectations, and over to God and your spouse. As a result, communication problems begin to improve, resentments fade away, and you naturally want to spend more time together. Of course, we can't expect such changes to happen overnight. It's a journey for sure. I'm still working on it after 43 years of marriage!

By committing your relationship to God and making a conscious decision each day to put God first and your spouse next, your marriage should be able to weather any storm. Look to Him as your anchor. Not only that, you'll also have plenty of fun together along the way!

Have you struggled to find happiness in your marriage? Perhaps it's time you and your spouse invited God to direct your relationship. I encourage you to pray the following:

Dear God, thank you so much for bringing us together as a couple. I know that You have a plan and a purpose for my marriage. Please forgive my past self-centeredness. I invite you into my marriage relationship, to direct our steps from now on. Please give us the grace to put You and each other first every day. Make our relationship a blessing to others. But most of all; make it a blessing to You. Amen.

ARE YOU A SERVANT LOVER?

DEBBY SIBERT

"Let each of you look not only to his own interests, but also to the interests of others. Have this mind among yourselves, which is yours in Christ Jesus, who, though he was in the form of God, did not count equality with God a thing to be grasped, but emptied himself, by taking the form of a servant, being born in the likeness of men."

— PHILIPPIANS 2:3-7 (ESV)

What does it take to be a servant lover? The way that God usually develops our integrity is to put people in our lives who tempt us to express the exact opposite quality. Character development involves choices and opposition provides those opportunities. Unfortunately, conflict seems inevitable in a marriage relationship. How do you handle that and what are you doing to foster an atmosphere of service one to another?

My husband and I independently decided early on in our marriage that we would be a student of each other – to learn what each other like and dislike and to use that information for good and not for evil! Our pastor asked us recently, "Are you intentionally striving to 'out-serve' one another?" At least for me, this kind of serving does not come naturally, so I have had to become more purposeful in how I live my life.

I developed a "self-assessment" checklist for both husbands and wives. See how you're doing in the serving area. I use this daily as an attempt to keep myself on track.

BOTH HUSBAND AND WIFE:

- Am I living intentionally, to seek and serve the best interests of my spouse, putting his/her needs before mine?
- Am I seeking to serve rather than to be served?
- Am I focusing on the positives in my spouse and how I can support him/her by building them up and showing respect and gratitude for what they bring to our relationship?
- Do I praise my spouse in public whether or not they are present?
- Have I created a comfortable, orderly, peaceful environment in our home, so that it is a safe haven for our family to enjoy?
- Do I praise good behavior? Am I a peacemaker?
- Do I have the maturity to always take the high road and do the right thing (rather than retaliating) even if my spouse is acting poorly and/or being immature at the moment?
- Do I freely and frequently extend grace and forgiveness when called for and leave any vengeance to God?
- Do I make sure that I am not keeping an account of wrongs?

- Am I seeking to love my spouse using *his/her* love language?
- Do I value our relationship and my commitment to my spouse over being right and/or getting my way?
- Have I convinced my spouse that I trust their heart and am committed to them for life no matter what life throws at us?

WIFE:

- Do I seek to resolve conflict biblically and lovingly submit to my husband's authority as the head of our household?
- Have I resolved to meet my husband's sexual needs even if I am not interested, too tired, etc.? Do I affirm him?
- Does my husband feel desired by me and do I make a point of doing things with him that he enjoys for companionship?

HUSBAND:

- Do I seek to resolve conflict biblically and lovingly and selflessly exercise my authority as the head of our household?
- Do I provide my wife with non-sexual touch and affection as well as seek to ensure that she also experiences pleasure in our lovemaking? Do I affirm and listen to her?
- Does my wife feel desired by me and do I make a point of doing things with her and for her? Do I share my thoughts and feelings? Am I a good listener?

How did you do?

Oh Lord, I see so many areas where I fall short in serving my spouse. Please instill in me a desire to make the necessary changes to "out-serve" my spouse to Your glory and may others see You at work in our marriage as we strive to emulate Christ and His church. May we be an example of your character and an extension of your grace and love to one another. Amen.

COMMUNICATION, COMMUNICATION, COMMUNICATION

DEBBY SIBERT

"Let every person be quick to hear, slow to speak, slow to anger."

— JAMES 1:19B (ESV)

"Let your speech always be gracious, seasoned with salt, so that you may know how you ought to answer each person."

— COLOSSIANS 4:6 (ESV)

You've probably heard that the three most important words in real estate are location, location, location. Well, my experience has shown that the three most important words in marriage are communication, communication, communication. Most marital issues seem to stem from some breakdown in that area.

Just as there are gender differences in how we see, hear and feel things, we all seem to have different ways in which we process our communication, which are often unhelpful. We most probably have married someone with the opposite default responses to issues in how we respond.

A breakthrough came to me when I discovered that my goal and that of my husband in communication should be to come to a mutual understanding, recognizing that we are not each other's enemy, but we should be allies. We are a team. We must realize that communication is more what's heard than what's said, so we need to be careful *how* we say *what* we say. What is our tone? We cannot "unring" a bell, so it's best to *taste* our words before spewing them out.

To quote Stephen Covey from his book, *Seven Habits of Highly Effective People*, he said, "Seek first to understand, and then to be understood." Words are powerful. In a moment they can heal but they also can destroy.

With which method of communication during conflict do you most identify? Do you withdraw, escalate, negatively interpret, or invalidate? Most likely you fall in one of these categories. Let's look at each of these.

Withdraw: trying to avoid conflict and unwilling to stick with an important discussion. Often referred to as placating, this is someone who wants peace at all costs and will say anything to avoid an argument. I hate to admit, this is where I struggle.

> *A better way*—If you need time to process, tell your spouse you need some time, but be willing to come back together to bring closure to the issue.

Escalate: When an argument gets heated and voices rise. It might show up as sarcasm, name calling or even threats. This can get ugly very quickly, especially if reciprocated.

> *A better way*—If you feel rage coming upon you, suggest a "time-out" for a period of time and separate to pray about your response and come back together after a designated time to amicably discuss the issue at hand.

Negatively Interpret: This happens when a negative motive has been assigned to an issue, or there are assumptions that things are more negative than they really are.

> *A better way*—Assume best intentions. If you need clarification, ask for it, but don't just assume a negative motive.

Invalidate: dismissing or minimizing, or putting down the thoughts, feelings or even the character of the other person.

> *A better way*—Be respectful of your spouse's thoughts, feelings, and concerns. You don't have to agree with them, but it is important that they feel valued and understood.

The way we communicate with our spouse can have a huge impact on the quality of a marriage. Communication is an opportunity to honor God and do everything you can to "live peaceably" with your spouse.

Oh Lord, how I thank You for the gift of my spouse. May my speech bring healing and not hurt. May it build up and not tear down. May my words foster peace and not pain. May it be seasoned with grace, mercy and love; and may I live with my spouse in an understanding way such that You are honored and I have no regrets. Amen.

THE HEALING POWER OF FORGIVENESS

DEBBY SIBERT

"Put on then, as God's chosen ones, holy and beloved,
compassionate hearts, kindness, humility, meekness,
and patience, bearing with one another and, if one has
a complaint against another, forgiving each other; as
the Lord has forgiven you, so you also must forgive.
And above all these put on love, which binds
everything together in perfect harmony. And let the
peace of Christ rule in your hearts, to which indeed
you were called in one body. And be thankful."

— COLOSSIANS 3:12-15 (ESV)

What is forgiveness? It's giving up the right to hurt you for hurting me. When we forgive, we emulate the very character of God because that is one of his greatest attributes.

The power to forgive is one of the most amazing gifts that God gives us. This couldn't be more applicable than in marriage. Forgiveness can transform our marriages and is a choice we have—to love, rather than to demand justice. Although we can't help but experience that indwelling desire to get even, we can respond with a more powerful desire for reconciliation. Marriage teaches us how to forgive because it provides so many opportunities to practice forgiveness which is a process—a journey, not an event.

When we got married, my husband and I wrote our own vows based on scripture. When we shared them on our wedding day, our pastor said, "You have made some wonderful promises to each other, but I must warn you that you will not be able to keep them all. One thing you must do is to learn and be willing to ask for and grant forgiveness freely and often." What wonderful advice that we have taken to heart which has served us well all these years.

Love keeps no record of wrongs. While it may seem humanly impossible to love this way, we can choose to give up our rights to hang on to the past and to rise above that with an attitude to persevere and keep moving forward— keeping our eyes on Jesus, our perfect example of forgiveness. Once an issue has been dealt with and forgiveness exchanged, it is important to move on and not dwell on past wrongs. Let it go and don't go dredging it up again later. Learning how to say we're sorry and to freely extend forgiveness to one another is central for marital peace.

You may not feel like forgiving at first. That's okay. It is a decision – an act of the will. It means letting go of the past. Your feelings will follow. It is said that "It's easier to act your way into feelings than to feel your way into acting." Forgiving is more powerful when it is least deserved or expected.

It does not mean that you have to pretend that nothing happened. You probably will not be able to forget about what happened, but when forgiveness has taken place, the emotions that come when you do think about it will be much different than before. You will be able to recall the event as something that happened in your past, yet the hurt is no longer there. On the other hand, hurts that are not dealt with and forgiven are stored in our subconscious memory as a negative emotion. That is why they must be dealt with. Acid tends to eat away at the container that stores it.

I have found so much truth in the saying that the one who benefits the most from forgiveness is not the one who receives it, but the one who grants it. Forgiveness cannot change your past, but it *can* change your future.

Oh Lord, forgiveness can be so hard. Please give me the grace to forgive my spouse when I feel I have been wronged, misunderstood, or hurt. You have forgiven me so much and I know I have no excuse not to pay forward the grace and mercy You have extended to me. Give me the courage also to ask for forgiveness when needed. I can't do this in my own efforts, so I pray for You to soften my heart towards my spouse and help us to reconcile our differences. Amen.

Debby Sibert is a mother of three married children and grandmother to nine. She and her husband of forty-three years, Bob, live in Northern Virginia. They worship and serve at McLean Bible Church.

Having come to Christ at a young age, she has been a Christ follower for over 60 years and student of the Bible for 50. Among other ministries in and outside her church, Debby is an inspirational speaker on faith, relationships, and insights concerning the abundant, victorious Christian life and has written several books to help Christians take their walk with God to the next level. She is also a Certified Christian Life Coach with an emphasis on Marriage Relationships.

debbysibert.com

CANNING THE COMPARISON

JACKIE PERSEGHETTI

"A heart at peace gives life to the body, but envy rots the bones."

— PROVERBS 14:30 (NIV)

*C*omparison. We all tend to do it, whether it's comparing our past to our current situation, our marriage to another couple's, or even where we are to where we dreamt we'd be. Even the psalmist wasn't immune when he compared: "*They* have no struggles; *their* bodies are healthy and strong. *They* are free from the burdens common to man; *they* are not plagued by human ills." (Psalm 73: 4-5 NIV, emphasis mine)

While it might seem the psalmist was comparing his marriage to another's, he was actually comparing his efforts to live for God with the wicked's habit to live for himself. And the grass was beginning to look greener on the other side of the fence.

No surprise there. When our eyes are busy looking to our left and right, they are automatically diverted from looking up at God. And our vision soon becomes fixated on an unsatisfiable inward focus. "Why does *he/she* have all the breaks?" "I wish my mate was more like...." "If only I had..." "Life will be better when..."

In my own experience, comparison and entrapment are tied at the hip. Comparison causes my eyes to wander, and my heart to stray. Once my heart strays, I become entrapped. Comparison and entrapment have more in common than just some letters they share in their spelling. The shared letters of M, P, A, R, N can easily stand for: M (Misery); P (Poisonous thoughts); A (Anger); R (Restlessness); N (Negative outcomes).

I feel miserable and fall prey to a discontent heart; nothing will please it. And that leads to poisonous thoughts of "my mate ain't that great," which turns into a low boil of anger over unmet expectations that I unfairly place on my spouse. And when those unmet expectations seem continual? My heart grows restless, and I begin making poor choices with negative outcomes, harming my spouse and myself.

Interestingly, in Psalm 73 the psalmist sees his potential comparison catastrophe: "But as for me, my feet had almost slipped; I had nearly lost my foothold. For I envied the arrogant when I saw the prosperity of the wicked."

In verses 21-26 we learn he had a hard time with comparison – until he focused on God. In the midst of his lack (compared to others) he wrote: "When my heart was grieved and my spirit embittered, I was senseless and ignorant; I was a brute beast before you. YET I am always with you; you hold me by my right hand. You guide me with your counsel, and afterward you will take me into glory. Whom have I in heaven but you? And earth has nothing I desire besides you. My flesh and my heart may fail, but God is the strength of my heart and my portion forever."

What is the cure to stop comparison? The psalmist shows us it's practicing a heart of gratitude toward God – whether we're living in plenty or in want. This gives us a heart at peace. Peace (*Shalom* in Hebrew) doesn't depend upon circumstances. It means "wholeness; completeness; everything being as God originally intended it to be." It is a God-focused and God-given gift that breathes life down into the deepest, darkest corners of our hearts, and delivers us from entrapment as we learn to can the comparison.

Lord, my insecure heart reaches for fulfillment in things I don't have, or things I want that others have. When I don't feel I have enough, my wandering heart fills with discontent and resentment. Please forgive me for not finding my fulfillment in You. You are a good God. Help me to live in the reality the psalmist discovered when he concluded, "But as for me, it is good to be near God. I have made the Sovereign Lord my refuge..."

THE COURAGEOUS ASK

JACKIE PERSEGHETTI

*"Whether we are adulterers or thoughtless spouses, the problem with all of us is that we stubbornly regard our interpersonal failures not as **inexcusably selfish choices**, but as **understandable mistakes**. The things our spouses do to us seem more like the former; the things we do to them, more like the latter..."*

— DR. LARRY CRABB, *MEN AND WOMEN: ENJOYING THE DIFFERENCE*

I grew up with performance based love and a perfectionist tendency followed me into our marriage. If I saw a flaw in my own character, by hook or crook I was going to work on it. And I did.

Sure, I failed and also flailed in my flaws, but those were easily excusable – understandable mistakes. I was tired, or felt stretched to the max, or perhaps even "hangry." Perhaps my blood sugars were out of whack, or my hormones off. It may have been our children arguing, or even the predictable fact that I was interrupted – yet again.

I could come up with a myriad of excuses, but the simple truth was, I was battling with my own selfishness. Marriage has a (God-designed) way of bringing our selfishness to the surface. And we have a myriad of ways for excusing our own behavior. "They were merely understandable mistakes we made. We really aren't *that* person."

Or are we?

Why do we excuse our own behavior while applying harsher standards toward our spouse? I believe it's because selfishness desires comfort. It has demands that crave immediate satisfaction. And its demanding nature has low tolerance for those that don't step up to the plate or perform with perfection.

A recent example of this is the folded piles of clothes at the foot of my bed—my ~~pile~~ *piles*, and my husband's single pile. My plan is to *someday* go through my piles, deciding what to keep and what to donate to Goodwill. My husband's pile is just a few folded clothes waiting to be put away from the dryer. While peering over my multiple mountains of procrastination one day, I viewed his little mound as a monument to his laziness. I readily excused my own lack of action and quickly grew frustrated at his. My inaction was understandable; his wasn't. I was in the right; he was in the wrong. Really?!

I really was being "*that* person."

Dr. Larry Crabb addresses our tendency toward self-justification with words of truth and hope:

"*More than anything else, what gets in the way of getting along is self-centeredness that seems reasonable.* God does his deepest work in making us more truly loving when we more clearly see how utterly ugly our selfishness is."

In my marriage, I've found that facing selfishness and confronting the temptation to dismiss my own sin takes courage. It also takes the Lord. I simply can't live *for* God *without* Him. There are two types of courageous asks: the first one is asking my spouse for forgiveness when I'm operating in selfishness; the second one is asking God to change me.

> *"If we confess our sins, he is faithful and just and will forgive us our sins and purify us from all unrighteousness."*
>
> — 1 JOHN 1:9 (NIV)

What unrighteousness in your own life needs His forgiveness and healing touch? Tell Him about it. What do you need to ask your spouse's forgiveness for? Make a point to do it. Today. Asking for forgiveness goes beyond stating "I'm sorry." It is admitting a specific action or attitude, saying why it was wrong, and then inviting the other person into the completion of the restorative process by humbly asking, "Will you forgive me?"

"WATERING" YOUR SPOUSE

JACKIE PERSEGHETTI

"A garden requires patient labor and attention. Plants do not grow merely to satisfy ambitions or to fulfill good intentions. They thrive because someone expended effort on them."

— LIBERTY HYDE BAILEY

I've killed one too many (actually all) of the succulent houseplants I've ever owned. They are either overwatered rotting mounds, or neglected shriveled up corpses. While some consider succulents easy to care for, I consider them fussy and requiring thoughtfulness. When I water my other plants (all doing quite well, thank you) I have to skip watering the succulents, because they like their soil "drier." Sometimes I forget to come back and check on them. Other times, I assume they're fine and don't water them for months.

Our spouses are like plants. Their watering needs aren't always convenient – or remembered. And having moments of flooding them with too much water to "hold them over" to their next sporadic watering only waterlogs the soil and kills the roots.

Just because I might be a plant that thrives in sunny windows and can absorb volumes of water doesn't mean the same is good for my mate. I need to water him according to his needs, not my own. To do that well, I need to expend the energy to know, understand, observe, and serve him. It's not automatic. It's not half-hearted. It's loving and intentional effort.

When I am sensitive to the needs of my spouse, only then can I "water" him well.

Our culture doesn't make this easy, constantly bombarding us with demands, distractions, and obligations to the point of mental overwhelm and emotional fatigue. We're daily tempted with the daydream of living with fake plastic houseplants that only need dusting once or twice a year and can be ignored at will.

But that's not real. And it isn't rewarding. What is real and rewarding is getting our hands dirty. It's the joy of learning as we go, and appreciating the mystery and wonder of our mate. It's putting value in what is truly valuable, and not being content to just coexist under the same roof. It's the opportunity to experience the joy of change and growth – in both our spouse and ourselves.

So what does watering our spouses well entail? Here are some ideas in seed form to help you:

W—Wisdom: Seek God's wisdom. The Lord made your spouse, and He knows the depths of his/her soul. Ask Him to simply show you how to love your mate well. (See James 1:5)

A—Admiration: Admire the good things you see in your spouse, and let him/her know about them. (See Philippians 4:8)

T—Together Time: Find what is meaningful and soul refreshing to your spouse, and plan time to do it together.

E—Engagement: When your spouse is talking to you, give eye-contact. Stop what you are doing to really listen to what he/she has to say. (See James 1:19-20)

R—Reset: When frustration rises in your heart, surrender it to the Lord and ask Him to change you. We become angry not because of a circumstance, but because of what's inside our own hearts. Part of being married is the Lord nurturing and watering *us* as we learn and grow through marriage. (See James 4:1-3, 10)

When we begin to acknowledge the uniqueness of our spouse, we begin to understand the beauty and joy of watering well.

Lord, I confess there are times when I've chosen to water my mate in convenient or lazy ways. I haven't always appreciated or nurtured the gift of my spouse whom You have given me. Please forgive me, Lord, and help me to be who you want me to be in his/her life. I can't do this without your help and strength. So right here, right now, I surrender my pride and self-sufficiency. Water my own soul with your Truth, and give me the strength, desire, and wisdom to "water" my mate well.

WHEN UNITY ROUTS UNIFORMITY

JACKIE PERSEGHETTI

"Unity, not uniformity, must be our aim. We attain unity only through variety. Differences must be integrated, not annihilated, not absorbed."

— MARY PARKER FOLLETT, (1918)

*M*arriage is a warzone revealing enemy combatants and secret spies hidden deep within our souls. Our enemy is not who we think it is (our mate), but rather something much more commanding, unpredictable, and calculated.

I still remember all the beauty and feels of our wedding day nearly 40 years ago. *"Together we walk life's path to what God has prepared for us"* boldly declared our direction, and the song, *"As One,"* gave testimony to the desire and intention of our hearts.

While none of that has changed, married life over the years has changed us.

Yes, there have been many times when I've marched forward, waving the flag of my opinion and expecting my spouse to fall in line. There have also been moments when I grew discouraged because he seemed to be following a different battle plan than my own. If we were going to be an effective squadron for the Lord, we needed to wear the same uniform, have the same passion, and see things the same way, I thought.

I mistook uniformity for unity, and the two are nowhere near the same.

Uniformity grasps at control, while unity hands out freedom. Uniformity compares and passes judgment, while unity considers, then offers grace. Uniformity is like wearing a stiff uniform; unity is donning a flowing cape that can accommodate various shapes and sizes.

I remember when I first faced the enemy combatant spy hidden deep within my soul. Its name was Control, and it secretly sought to be commander. I desired my husband and I to march in lock-step because I thought that's how every good marriage should be. We should have the same passions, like the same foods, and share the same interests. Certainly, our walk with the Lord should be expressed in similar ways in order for us to be "as one." I became inwardly frustrated and even fearful when he did things differently. *Treason!* My heart silently screamed. The spies of Comparison, Control, Fear, Insecurity, Pride joined the battle, with the ammunition of criticism and correction aimed at my spouse. They were there to reinforce uniformity at the call of the commander, Self. They were relentless warriors, but they were not undefeatable.

I wish I could say I dispatched those enemy combatants early in my marriage, but that would be lying. And to be honest, there are still times when they try to sneak their way back into the command post. But now I know the enemy is not my spouse or even differences between us. I have seen the enemy, and it is within me.

Our battle is not for uniformity, but for unity—and that battle is only won when we follow our Commander in Chief, the Lord. Yes, marriage will always be a warzone as we battle to keep the right Commander in charge and rout out those secret spies hidden deep within our souls. But the good news is when we follow the Lord, we get to celebrate walking victoriously in new places of freedom.

> *"Make my joy complete by being like-minded, having the same love, being one in spirit and of one mind. Do nothing out of selfish ambition or vain conceit. Rather, in humility value others above yourselves, not looking to your own interests but each of you to the interests of the others."*
>
> — EPHESIANS 2:2-4 (NIV)

Complete this prayer, inviting God into your mess. Ask Him for His help and thank Him for His compassion: "Lord, You know how often I ..."

Jackie Perseghetti is a bestselling Author, educator, speaker, and mentor whose passion is to breathe life into the hearts of the weary so they can walk in new places of simplicity, freedom, and authenticity with God. From writing best-selling devotional—one selling over a quarter of a million copies—to having her work published in *The Godly Businesswoman*, *Clubhouse*, and *Evangelizing Today's Child* magazines, Jackie continues to encourage, teach, and inspire those who read her work.

In her down time, you can find Jackie playing pickleball, sneaking a piece of dark chocolate, or stopping in the middle of a walk to snap that perfect nature shot with her cell phone. She enjoys going on "adfuntures" (adventure with fun in the middle) with Doug, her beloved husband of nearly 40 years, relaxing with their two rescue dogs, loving on their grandchildren, and opening their home with hospitality.

Connect with Jackie to be encouraged in the journey of cultivating an undivided heart, and find her on Instagram @jackieperseghetti.

akingdomheartbeat.com

amazon.com/stores/author/B0024JIAMU

TRANSFORMATION

BECKY SIMS

"We all, with unveiled faces, are looking as in a mirror at the glory of the Lord and are being transformed into the same image from glory to glory; this is from the Lord who is the Spirit."

— 2 CORINTHIANS 3:18 (HCSB)

Transformation: this is the word my family chose for 2022.

"Transformation" reminds me of God's plan for the butterflies—how they start their lives as caterpillars, spin a chrysalis, and emerge as beautiful flying creatures!

Marriage often involves transformation on various levels through a variety of circumstances. Each situation brings its very own set of challenges and opportunities.

A transformation my husband and I are currently walking through is the loss of his parents and settling their estate, including selling his childhood home. We are also sending our younger son to college this fall, moving us closer to the empty nest stage.

Since my husband and I are celebrating our 30th anniversary this year, we are reflecting on what we have already done and how we want to transform as we continue in our married life. We plan to have more dates and dreaming sessions that will bring us closer together and help us focus on what matters most. In Romans 12:2 Paul encourages everyone to be transformed by the renewing of our minds so we can discern the good, pleasing, and perfect will God has for our lives. No matter what's going on in our lives, if we listen to the Lord and follow His plans, He will transform us to be who He has created us to be! What areas of your life could use a transformation in the coming year?

Dear Lord, thank You for helping us to transform throughout our journey. Please help us to seek You in all areas and to strive to give You first place in our lives. We long to be who You created us to be! In Christ's name, Amen.

DATES AND DREAMS

BECKY SIMS

"Then the Lord God said, 'It is not good for the man to be
alone. I will make a helper as his complement.'"
"So the Lord God caused a deep sleep to come over the
man, and he slept. God took one of his ribs and closed
the flesh at that place. Then the Lord God made the
rib He had taken from the man into a woman and
brought her to the man. And the man said: 'This one,
at last, is bone of my bone and flesh of my flesh; this
one will be called "woman," for she was taken from
man." This is why a man leaves his father and mother
and bonds with his wife, and they become one flesh."

— GENESIS 2:18, 21-24 (HCSB)

While riding home one night, my mind
wandered to why my husband and I haven't
been spending much quality time alone together. We have
meals together as a family and spend the majority of our
days at home together. And yet, the talking we do always
seems to focus on tasks at hand and our current

responsibilities. The days just blur together in a pattern of routine and quick recovery operations, resulting in a lack of joy in our marriage relationship.

God created men and women to become helpmates and marriage partners for life. He designed us each to be uniquely gifted to fit together as one, with Him as the center. It seems we often forget the blessings of this unity when life becomes routine or overwhelming.

DATES

When I remember my dating days, I picture the times together with only the one I loved. It didn't matter if we were watching a movie, talking over dinner, or taking a walk. The joy was in being together. The art of dating doesn't go away once we are married. We need to remember to date our spouse. It might be completing a fun project together, going on a new adventure, or simply looking for small ways to express love. What is most important, however, is putting time and energy into honoring that time together.

DREAMS

Dreams remind me of my wedding day. My husband and I stated our vows to love, honor, and cherish one another until death. As newlyweds we were full of ideas and hopes of what our lives together would be like. We dreamed of where we wanted to live, how many kids we wanted to have, and even where we wanted to vacation or one day retire. We believed the best in each other and found it easy to overlook the flaws.

Dating comes first; dreaming comes second. If we don't feel loved, heard, and connected by our partner, we won't be able to dream with them. When thinking into the future, we can seek ways to keep our married lives interesting and focused on God first and one another second, which will keep our marriages thriving.

How is your dating and dreaming going? Why not plan some times for dates and dreams with your spouse? Do things that you both enjoy and appreciate the opportunity to talk and spend time together. Schedule a time to dream with each other about your future. Pray together and ask the Lord to continue to guide your marriage.

Dear Lord, thank You for designing the bond of marriage. Thank You for the opportunity to share our lives with our spouse, and to work together to create a life worthy of Your calling. Please help us to remember to take time for dating and dreaming with our partner so that we can keep our connection strong. In Christ's name, Amen.

CONFLICT RESOLUTION

BECKY SIMS

"Walk worthy of the calling you have received, with all
humility and gentleness, with patience, accepting one
another in love, diligently keeping the unity of the
Spirit with the peace that binds us."

— EPHESIANS 4:1B-3 (HCSB)

*E*ven after being married for over half of our lives,
my husband and I still don't agree or even
understand what each other is trying to say at times.

We are often so busy, it's more like we're "spitting"
information at each other as we're passing by. Sometimes
we'll raise our voices "just to be heard" over the other.
When I say we're arguing, he'll say we're not. And then we
both stop really listening to what the other says because
we don't feel validated.

Christian counselors often suggest communication can
be improved by taking turns listening to each other,
without interruption, followed by repeating what we think
we've heard before we begin to ask clarifying questions.

Sometimes, we forget our questions and talking points by the time it's our turn to share!

We tend to agree on the major topics that cause issues for many in their marriages. Our parenting styles and spending habits are in alignment. We have similar traditions and enjoy many of the same activities in our free time. But there are times when we seem to lose the peace, patience, and unity that comes with humility, gentleness, and diligence.

Marriages will have conflicts.

We will have disagreements and misunderstandings. I've personally found that because my husband and I are so closely connected, it hurts deeply to be misunderstood and have conflict between us.

By spending time in prayer, both alone and in unison, we can strengthen our spiritual bond and increase our ability to show love and respect for one another. Why not take some time to create a list of things you are grateful for in your spouse? When the conflicts come, remember the blessings you have shared. Give each other a little space and time when needed before addressing any conflicts.

Dear Lord, it can sometimes seem difficult living together with a spouse. We desire for our relationship to be connected and easy, but there are struggles. Lord, You understand each of us and we have committed ourselves to lovingly be there for one another. Help us to keep our relationship with You first. Please help us see our spouses through Your eyes and listen with Your ears and heart. In Christ's name, Amen.

SHARING SPACE

BECKY SIMS

*"And be kind and compassionate to one another, forgiving
one another, just as God also forgave you in Christ."*

— EPHESIANS 4:32 HCSB

I often joke that the only reason my husband and
I are still together is that we keep running into
each other! We seem to need to be in the same space many
times a day. Whether it's our closet, a cabinet, or at the
refrigerator, we meet up at the same place at the same
time, but need different things!

Sharing space with others isn't easy, but the blessings
that come with sharing our lives make it worthwhile.
There is comfort in having someone so close who knows
all about us and loves us anyway. We're able to help each
other through the difficulties and enjoy fun activities
together. Yet this togetherness can be frustrating at times.

Instead of focusing on the frustration of momentary
inconveniences, we can turn these moments around.
Rather than being in a taking mode, we can choose to give.

Our giving will be different depending on the situation. We might speak kind words instead of what is on the tips of our tongues, or we may offer a hug rather than a cold shoulder. We bless each other when we take time to remember the positives in our relationships and use these close encounters as opportunities to connect with one another.

I've personally found it a blessing to have some things my husband and I do separately. It makes our times together so much sweeter. This weekend, I had a solo writing retreat at a hotel. My husband had the house all to himself. It was a small break for both of us. But when I return home later today, we will have a renewed appreciation for each other and may even celebrate when our paths collide.

How do you share space with your spouse? In what ways can you adjust your interactions to strengthen your marriage and renew your appreciation for each other?

Dear Lord, thank you for creating marriage and for the opportunity to share our lives as husband and wife. Please help us to live with peace, patience, and a gentle love. Remind us that You have brought us together for Your purpose and help us to keep You at the center of our relationship. In Christ's name, Amen.

Becky Sims has a strong faith in Jesus and a love for writing encouraging letters to friends and others. She prays that her devotional blog and books will help other women longing to grow closer to the Lord to gain hope and meaning in their lives, while looking forward with confidence to eternity in heaven.

Becky is a wife and mother, Hope*Writer, former teacher, and author. She is active in her church choir. She especially enjoys quiet time with the Lord and often spends time on her porch chair in prayer.

amazon.com/Becky-Sims/e/B08ZM13DV4/

beckysims.org

FOR FOODIES ONLY

MIRANDA J. CHIVERS

"Better a serving of vegetables with love than a fattened calf with hatred."

— PROVERBS 15:17 (NIV)

This passage reminds us that mealtime should be respectful and shared in an atmosphere of love. There's no joy in dining on meat that's drowning in a gravy of hatred. But a passionate meal prepared by two tender hands with a gentle heart perfumes the air with kindness and forgiveness.

Eating when we're angry is unhealthy. Stress interferes with digestion and sleep. And who wants to sit at the table with an enemy? But there's more to chew on here.

Food is a powerful symbol that suggests an intimate gathering containing emotional elements. We can dress it up or keep it simple, but either way — whether eating alone, or with spouse, family or friends, this time is to be cherished. What's on the menu isn't as important as how it's served and who it's shared with.

When cooked with love, good food is a panacea. Although chicken soup doesn't really heal anything per se, it makes us feel better — if only for a little while. And when it's delivered by a caring friend, we feel loved.

In my Russian-Ukrainian Mennonite community, the female elders held to the adage "the way to a man's heart is through his stomach."

This phrase adds to the above proverb by suggesting that food is a cure-all, a type of band-aid that fixes bad moods and sad hearts. I was taught that if a man eats well at home, he won't visit another woman's "kitchen." If he does stray, he'll come back—because the best cook still lives at the house he built.

There may be a grain of truth in this, but there's more to roast here.

Growing up, the dinner bell stopped many arguments between my brothers and me, and gave us an hour to reflect on why we were upset. Since grumpiness at the table was forbidden, this gave us the opportunity to smooth the family waters with more pleasant talk. If mom sensed that anger was still hanging in the air, she'd bring out her famous apple pie with double scoops of ice cream. Perhaps she knew that sugar raises the dopamine and serotonin levels — two hormones that make us feel satisfied and happy.

After supper, it was the men's job to clean the grill and sweep the floor. The conflict was forgotten temporarily. But when the heat's left on the grill, the grunge burns. And dirt has a sneaky way of coming back. Since we didn't remove the bone of contention from the broth of our sibling relationship, resentment baked. The competition continued. In the end no one won.

In marriage, I try to keep my beef with my husband until after dinner. Choosing the timing and place to have a difficult discussion is one key to keeping tempers cool. And menu choices can shift moods. But the danger here is still the same as the one I had with my brothers. Too much coddling becomes manipulation. And setting the timer for too long can overcook feelings, too.

Marriage shouldn't be a meal of leftovers meant for dogs. It's the most cherished relationship in life and it deserves the finest of dishes. But whatever you serve, keep your motives pure. And don't hesitate to end with a fancy dessert. Sugar helps heal the hurting heart.

Dear Lord, forgive me for being selfish and giving my spouse the leftovers from my heart. He deserves honesty and clear communication, but also the best of my talents.

EXPECTATIONS IN MARRIAGE

MIRANDA J. CHIVERS

*"Get rid of all bitterness, rage and anger, brawling and
slander, along with every form of malice. Be kind and
compassionate to one another, forgiving each other,
just as in Christ God forgave you."*

— EPHESIANS 4:31-32 (NIV)

*M*arriage is full of complex emotions that rip
at our souls. Erasing negative feelings and
replacing them with loving kindness is easier said than
done because the root cause often lies deeper. Prayer is the
first step in self-examination. An honest reflection of our
mistakes helps us change our destructive behaviors.

Experts encourage us to focus on our compatibility,
improve communication skills, and practice forgiveness.
But apologizing or listening more effectively doesn't
overcome all disharmony. Since we come to this union
with our individual histories and unique cultural biases,
our perceptions and viewpoints often clash.

Although I have a background in social work, it's the forty-five years between two challenging marriages that taught me how family backgrounds, ideologies, and faith differences underlie miscommunications and disputes.

Both of my two husbands and I grew up in traditional families with patriarchal views of women and children, but we were immersed in a changing society that pushed against the status quo.

During this time, the pill was invented and sexual freedom became blatant. The law gave women property rights, no-fault divorce, and enforced child support. Although these changes made some things easier for women, these same policies were also used as weapons. Financial, physical, sexual, and emotional abuse were common both in homes and in the workplace.

These societal changes dramatically affected my generation and set up unparalleled expectations within marriage. Instead of our home being a refuge, it became a breeding ground for conflict. Not only were we struggling for equality in the workplace, we were also fighting to have our voice heard at home.

Even though things were changing, social support was not in place to protect women and children. And since family values shift over generations (not years), many women held onto the old viewpoints that encouraged dependence or resigned themselves to living in dysfunctional and abusive relationships.

My church's teachings plus the traditional beliefs of my family and our Eastern European culture disagreed with the new ideology. They insisted that a man's viewpoint was generally right and a woman was expected to defer to her husband.

Because of these distorted perspectives, I didn't use my voice to express my needs, and my self-esteem suffered.

Then, the respect within the relationship deteriorated. Communication became manipulative and abusive.

When a marriage deteriorates to this degree, it's difficult, but not impossible, to repair. The hard work comes in changing old patterns and regaining respect. Unfortunately, pride often impedes change and a partnership requires two to carry the heavy load.

In my Unequally Yoked Facebook marriage support group, I've noticed many still use certain Biblical texts to justify women staying in a sick marriage. But the Bible doesn't say that.

The Bible heralds healthy relationships that emphasize the importance of respect and grace. Jesus's discussion with the woman at the well encouraged her self-esteem and offered better options to her broken life. Similarly, the woman who touched the hem of his garment didn't need more condemnation. She needed healing.

Likewise, dysfunctional marriages need spiritual rehabilitation. Uncovering the source of the heartache is less painful when we approach each other with respect, grace, and open communication. Understanding our differences from new perspectives helps us appreciate why we fell in love at the start. Then forgiveness enters. And marriage begins anew.

Heavenly Father, show me the resentments that I'm holding against my spouse. Give me wisdom to see things from your perspective. Help me to boldly ask for what I need when I need it; and please guide me to listen more effectively, be kinder and more forgiving.

RECONSTRUCTION

MIRANDA J. CHIVERS

*"Do not merely listen to the word, and so deceive
yourselves. Do what it says."*

— JAMES 1:22 (NIV)

*M*y best advice for newlyweds is this: love
unconditionally, listen well, and forgive
always.

Those words may seem redundant to newly marrieds.
But those with experience know how quickly rose-colored
glasses shatter. When prickly situations trigger that old
chip on our shoulder or our pride gets hurt, these well-
worn phrases suddenly become impossible tasks.

And when tempers are hot, it's tempting to play the
blame game and avoid looking at ourselves.

We come into marriage with old patterns of relating
and with cultural biases from our family of origin. The
model of marriage ingrained in our subconscious came
from our parents. We grew up with their know-how and
learned our conflict resolution skills from them. So, if they

had a healthy marriage and our home was well-adjusted, then we're better prepared to handle the stresses of an intimate relationship. But if it wasn't, then eventually we'll find ourselves overwhelmed.

If both spouses are Christ followers, there's an expectation that faith and love conquers all. But here again, preparation and implementation are keys. Faith is a good connection point to fix what's broken. But putting Christ's words into practice isn't as easy as it sounds, especially when one or both partners have grown up in a dysfunctional home.

If my foundation is damaged, then it needs rebuilding. It's wiser to hire an experienced carpenter to supervise the work than to figure it all out myself.

Rebuilding from the ground up is hard work. Paint is pretty. But like nice words, it only covers up the rotten wood for a short time. And, although praying for God's power to shed light in the darkness is helpful and necessary during tough times, skill sets such as communication, belief systems, and behavioral patterns may still need re-tuning. In other words, it's not what you know, it's how you put it into practice that matters. And that's where a counselor or marriage coach can help.

In my Unequally Yoked Marriage Support Facebook Group, I've noticed that it's often one spouse's lack of dedication to the Christian faith that pushes the other partner into seeking help. Sometimes a woman wonders if her husband is truly saved. He may not commit to the church calendar because he's too busy with work and day-to-day life. But she may feel he's drifting.

If one marriage partner is less serious about their faith than the other, the relationship may feel imbalanced. But this is seldom the only problem. We all have cracks in our foundation. And each person's faith grows at different rates.

The Bible teaches us to practice gentle encouragement and patience towards the weaker member to inspire the other.

But here's a key nugget: Being a Christian isn't about attending church, although this is vital for our growth. To embrace our faith, we must study the Word. This is a daily exercise requiring reading, meditation, chewing on and praying into passages that spark something in our soul. Only then can we implement the principles into our daily lives. Without this, we are just good people who want to do good works and who go to church. We must allow the Holy Spirit to change us from the inside.

And this brings us to the next key: We must be willing to change without expecting our spouse to do so as well. My spouse is not responsible for my spiritual life, nor my behavior. My salvation does not depend on his choices. God holds each accountable for themselves. Often, our healthy changes influence others positively.

God, I realize when my expectations exceed another's abilities, I'm creating friction in the relationship. Likewise, when old childhood hurts are triggered, I react in unhealthy ways. Help me overcome them. Mold my problem-solving styles to become positive and encouraging to my spouse.

Miranda J. Chivers is the award winning Christian author of *Unequally Yoked: Staying Committed to Jesus and Your Unbelieving Spouse* and other devotionals (as well as fiction). A survivor of C-PTSD and chronic pain, she's been married to her spiritually mismatched spouse for thirty-two years. Together, they've raised a blended family of four (including their two developmentally challenged adults). Inspired by her life journey, her writings relay the complex inter-weavings of faith and mental health in overcoming difficulties.

Her facebook group "Unequally Yoked Marriage Support Group" supports Christians struggling to balance faith and marriage to a non-Christian.

amazon.com/author/mirandajchivers
linktr.ee/mjkrausechivers

LETTING GO OF SELF

DVORA ELISHEVA

> *"Do nothing from selfish ambition or conceit, but in*
> *humility count others more significant than*
> *yourselves. Let each of you look not only to his own*
> *interests, but also to the interests of others. Have this*
> *mind among yourselves, which is yours in Christ Jesus,*
> *who... emptied himself ... and humbled himself ... to*
> *the point of death..."*

— PHILIPPIANS 2:3–5, 7, 9 (PARAPHRASED
FROM THE ESV)

I'd been married less than a year when it
happened. It was nothing remarkable in and of
itself. And yet, to this day I am still learning from it.

A friend had reminded me about an outing planned
with several women from our church. It was the last day to
register, and Sue wanted to know if I would be joining
them. I'd completely forgotten about it and hadn't had the
chance to discuss it with Rich, my husband. I knew we had
nothing planned for the upcoming weekend and was sure

he'd have no problem with my going. Hence my immediate reply, "Sure, count me in."

I had married at the age of 53 and was used to making all my own decisions. Before agreeing to go, it didn't cross my mind to ask Rich what he thought. Even when single, it had rarely occurred to me to pray and ask my Lord if He would be pleased with my choice.

Arriving home, Rich asked if I had a good visit with Sue. I began to share, and then added in passing, "By the way, she reminded me about the ladies' trip, and I told her I'd go."

Rich looked at me in silence. His answer was soft, but his eyes had a hurt look. "You did?"

"Did you make plans I didn't know about?" I asked. Rich sighed, and said, "No, no plans."

Suddenly I felt on the defensive, "I thought sure you would want me to go, so I told her yes."

Rich was quiet for a moment, and then replied, "Yes, I do want you to go. It will be nice and a good opportunity to get to know others. But we are married now. Don't you think I deserved the respect of being involved in your decision?"

Discussing things with my husband, to which I knew he would agree, seemed so insignificant. But not doing so had revealed a deeper problem. Searching my heart, I realized that I'd only been thinking about what I wanted, and I'd assumed my husband wanted the same thing. That day I experienced a new death to self.

Rich forgave me and I enjoyed the trip. But from then on, I made every effort to involve him in all my decisions. In so doing, I discovered what an amazing blessing it was to have someone on my side. Sometimes, when I was sure he would disagree with something I wanted to do, he would agree, and there were other times when he had an even better idea that proved to be beyond my hopes or expectations.

I have learned that there is no room for selfish assumptions in marriage. In humility, we must learn to consider our spouse as more important than ourselves, looking to their interests and not just our own. But as we empty ourselves and humble ourselves before our spouse, an amazing thing happens; we become closer to each other, and to our Lord.

Precious Savior, how often have I failed to honor and respect my spouse by involving him in my decisions. How many times have I looked to my own needs first, rather than his. Forgive me. Give me Your spirit of humility to be willing to empty myself and die to self for the sake of my husband and the health of our marriage. And Lord, help me to lay aside my independence, because I need You, and I need my spouse. In your name I pray. Amen.

TRUST GOD'S WORK IN YOUR SPOUSE

DVORA ELISHEVA

"For it is God who works in you, both to will and to work for his good pleasure."

— PHILIPPIANS 2:13

*M*y husband had not been well for some time, so you can imagine my inner turmoil when he told me he planned to run for a US congressional seat. Not feeling like the subject was open for discussion, I responded, "really?" Rich asked me to help design his website, and I did, but my heart was not in it. Looking at his physical limitations, I could only think, how on earth would he run for the US Congress? What had gotten into him?

I love and am committed to traditional marriage vows. Nevertheless, promising to cling to the other "for better or for worse, for richer or for poorer, in sickness and in health, to love and to cherish, till death do us part," is heavy stuff, particularly if one pays attention to the depth of meaning behind those words.

Rich and I had barely been married for a year when he began to suffer serious health issues. He'd already had trouble finding work, and now depression was a heavy cloud attacking us. Physical, emotional, and financial stresses were piling high. We were praying and trying to trust the Lord together. It wasn't easy. Suddenly, Rich had come up with an outrageous goal that seemed utterly unrealistic to me.

How many dreams have been squashed by a well-meaning spouse who just couldn't envision their partner's dream becoming a reality? I am so thankful that God stopped me in my tracks early on. It happened over a lunch date when Rich gently confronted me, "You don't have my back."

As Rich and I talked, I learned that he really had prayed much about this. He had done far more than I realized and been accepted as the congressional candidate for the Libertarian Party. As he shared, the Holy Spirit was whispering in my heart, *didn't you encourage Rich to dream big and seek the Lord to use him?*

With a repentant heart, I finally understood my husband's passion. I became his biggest supporter in spirit, word, and deed. He campaigned before hundreds of people and gained increasing media attention as the months passed. Rich encouraged others to pray for their nation and to choose a candidate who cared about the country and not power. When he unexpectedly died a few months before the elections, hundreds of people attended his funeral and many, who otherwise might not have ever had the opportunity, heard the gospel. Rich had a far more significant impact on people's lives than he would ever know. His example inspired another man to run and become elected for office in his state legislature.

Does your spouse have a dream – a really big dream – that you think is absurd, insane, or even crazy? You made a commitment to love and cherish him. Love doesn't consider its own needs. Cherishing someone means encouraging and supporting them—including their dreams and longings. Rather than putting them down, pray for them and ask God to open HIS good doors for this person to whom you've made a lifelong commitment. They can't do it without Him or without you.

Heavenly Father, thank you for our spouses. How often we have not been very supportive of their job, their hobby, their dreams, or their goals. Help us to trust the work of your Holy Spirit in them. Make us our spouse's biggest fan and supporter. Teach us what it means to truly cherish all of who our spouse is and longs to be. In Jesus Name, Amen.

My pen name is Dvora Elisheva, Hebrew for Deborah Elizabeth (my real name in English). An author, writer, and teacher, I seek to use my skills to encourage others find new hope and meaning in their Creator—the God of the Bible who never fails. I came to Israel in 1982 and live in beautiful Haifa, on the Mediterranean Sea. I enjoy blogging, writing faith-based articles, and have authored a memoir, *Connecting the Dots of a Disconnected Life: Hope for a Fractured Soul*. The focus of my writing, ultimately, is our great hope. In a way, much of my writing is an open diary of life experiences. I write to share the reason for the hope within me and pray my writing will be a blessing to you. You can contact me at dvora@hope-challenged.com.

hope-challenged.com

GUARDING AGAINST PRIDE

KATIE ARTHUR

> *"When you say 'I would never,' you're actually full of spiritual pride because you're saying 'I don't need God there'."*

— AUDREY MEISNER

The news left me shocked, hurt, and confused. My mind wrestled with the reality of what I thought was impossible. How could he be unfaithful to his wife? I'd heard stories of and known past church leaders who fell prey to this temptation, but I never thought it would be him. As grief overwhelmed me, pride stole its way into my heart. I would never be unfaithful in *my* marriage.

It wasn't long before my marriage faced the perfect storm. I was the sole breadwinner for our family, and became physically unhealthy from lack of sleep while working the night shift. My husband was a stay at home dad with our son. We almost never saw each other, let alone spent time together. I would finish the night shift, lead a women's Bible study, volunteer for a Christian organization, and come home to sleep before I had to do it all over again. While I was doing everything I thought God wanted me to do, my husband was wrestling with a crisis of faith.

Then, on Easter weekend, I asked "Are you still a Christian?" He replied "No." It stung and my eyes welled with tears as my cheeks burned with anger, hurt, and grief. Even though I saw this coming, nothing could have prepared me for this punch to the gut. As my world spun out of control, I found myself married but alone.

More distant from my husband than before, I sought solace in a male friend. As I shared my pain, I felt heard and loved. Pride whispered the lie that "I would never..." and I believed it. It wasn't long before I was making small compromises to keep feeling heard and loved. The more I felt it, the more my heart's desires grew unfaithful. I wrestled for several months trying to remain faithful to my marriage and still maintain a friendship I knew was dangerous. That's when I found myself unexpectedly sitting in a hospital room with my husband. In a matter of hours he was diagnosed with Diabetic Ketoacidosis and would have died by morning had he not come in.

Suddenly faced with the possible loss of my husband, I had to make a choice. If my marriage was worth fighting for, the other relationship had to end. My heart had to be completely and wholly devoted to loving my husband—in spite of any major worldview differences. I walked away from the other relationship.

When we presumptuously allow pride to find its way into our hearts and marriages, we invite sin with it. So many Christians believe they are immune to affairs of the heart and divorce. It's simply a lie pride tells us to believe.

When we embrace that lie, we sever our dependence on God. When we stop being dependent on God, we fall.

If we want to guard our marriages against affairs and divorce, we must first recognize we are not immune. Then, we must invite God to hold us up in our weakness.

Are there any areas in your marriage where you've allowed pride to say it could never be you? Confess this pride before the Lord and invite him to hold you up again.

TO THE SPIRITUALLY MISMATCHED SPOUSE

KATIE ARTHUR

"To the rest I say (I, not the Lord) that if any brother has a wife who is an unbeliever, and she consents to live with him, he should not divorce her. If any woman has a husband who is an unbeliever, and he consents to live with her, she should not divorce him. But if the unbelieving partner separates, let it be so."

— 1 CORINTHIANS 7:12-13, 15A ESV

stood in the driveway, darkness enveloping me. I made my decision. "Lord, if we divorce, let him be the one to leave me." It wasn't my most eloquent prayer, but it was a prayer of declaration back to God. After wrestling for a year or more with desires to divorce, I finally understood his call for me to stay married to my husband as long as my husband was willing to stay married to me.

My perspective on my marriage shifted radically that night as I not only heard God's desires for my marriage, but responded to it with a complete change of heart. I began to understand that my marriage wasn't meant to provide me with the perfect companion for life, but to launch me into growth in my walk with the Lord.

Gary Thomas writes "The important thing is to view the challenges of our particular life situation as a platform for growth."

Being married to an atheist has become the catalyst of my spiritual growth. I am learning to build a habit of persistence as I daily bring my husband's salvation before the Lord in prayer. I struggle so much with this because day-after-day prayers seem to go unanswered, but I know God is using it to grow me. Had I divorced my husband, I would be missing an opportunity to grow.

Sister or brother in Christ, you too may be walking in a spiritually mismatched marriage. Maybe when you and your spouse married neither of you were Christians, but now you've come to know the Lord. Or maybe like me, your spouse professed Christ when you met, but has since renounced his or her faith.

I do not know your journey, but I do know that if you're a Believer and your spouse is not, God desires good for your marriage just as he desires good for a marriage between two Believers. If you are feeling alone, lost, hopeless, and full of fear, I implore you to shift your perspective and consider what growth God might be calling you to in the midst of a difficult marriage.

Father, it wasn't supposed to be this way. This spiritual rift between my spouse and I leaves me hurting and hopeless. I know you desire good for our marriage. I know you desire restoration of what has been lost. I also know that in this place of hardship and suffering, you want to teach me. Open my eyes to see the growth opportunity that is before me and use my spiritually mismatched marriage to draw me closer to you. Amen.

I'm the wife of an atheist and mom of one very strong-willed, yet tender-hearted, little boy. After three years of walking around deeply wounded and grieving after my husband renounced his faith and walked away from the church, I am learning to ask hard questions, answer hard questions, and live a life of disciplined grace daily in the presence of the Lord. It is my hope to share with sisters in Christ the grace I have experienced, the hope that I cling to, and the joy I have found in life as a result.

BEWARE THE FOXES

MIMI KROGER

*"Catch all the foxes, those little foxes, before they ruin
the vineyard of love, for the grapevines are
blossoming!"*

— SONG OF SOLOMON 2:15 (NLT)

*S*ome may consider the fox to be rather cute,
boasting pointed ears and bushy tails. Let's put
their outward appearance aside for a moment and consider
their cunning nature and ability to feed on hard-earned
gardens and innocent prey.

You might be thinking, what do little foxes have to do
with my marriage? Let's redefine what a little fox might
represent when it comes to you and the person with whom
you devotedly said, "I do."

Perhaps, you've been deceived by the foxes, those little
foxes, that have come to devour the love in your marriage
and its ability to produce fruit and blossom.

This beloved one, is what a fox in your home might
look like:

When you've made a request more than once—ok, maybe it's been 100 times by now.

When you've despised the sight of toothpaste that's drizzled on the bathroom counter because the cap wasn't put back on—again.

When they didn't call to let you know they'd be late for dinner—the very one you timed just perfectly so the buttery vegetables would be ready right alongside the main dish.

Did I mention this happened twice this week alone?

Interesting that the foxes are mentioned more than once in the Scripture: "the foxes, those little foxes." I believe it's because God knew it would be relatively easy to overlook the first offense.

It's when the fox has repeatedly come for a visit in our personal vineyard of love that our ability to let go of our annoyance becomes more difficult over time.

God invites us to do as His Word says in Philippians 4:8 (NLT), "And now, dear brothers and sisters, one final thing. Fix your thoughts on what is true, and honorable, and right, and pure, and lovely, and admirable. Think about things that are excellent and worthy of praise. Think on these things."

During times of frustration, our decision to focus on what our spouse *is doing right* rather than giving attention to the little foxes aligns us with the heart of God. We can place our trust in the Lord to bring life to our relationships so they can flourish into a garden of excellent love. Our own efforts to control and produce the changes we desire, in those nearest to our hearts, is usually ineffective and rather exhausting. As we place our trust in God, through prayer, He will prove His good nature as *He* divinely Fathers each of us into honoring and loving one another.

Father, thank you for being the Master Gardener. Help me to remain undistracted from the little foxes, keeping my focus on all that is good in our family garden, while I trust in You to keep its gates secure with Your faithfulness and provision for our heart's desires.

Mimi Kroger is a bestselling author, speaker, nationally certified personal trainer, nutrition guide, and behavior change specialist with a passion for health and wellness. She directs her clients toward healing rooted in a relationship with the Holy Spirit through the wisdom, guidance, and comfort He provides.

Mimi is the founder of 3 John 2 Ministries, a faith-based non-profit organization, with a mission to equip individuals on how to connect with the Holy Spirit, nourish their souls through that connection, and heal physical disease or emotional dis-*ease* as a result. Mimi enjoys being a mom to an amazing adult son. She resides in Colorado with her loving husband, Ben. They have a tenacious Yorkie named Hugs!

healthyhappyandheavenly.com

TWO ARE NOW ONE

ROBERT KAPEN

"Don't be selfish; don't try to impress others. Be humble, thinking of others as better than yourselves. Don't look out only for your own interests, but take an interest in others, too."

— PHILIPPIANS 2:3-4 (NLT)

I'm not an expert. I've only been married for a little over seven years, but what I have learned is that there are no perfect spouses. No one will check all the boxes all the time because we are all flawed human beings. Even though marriage involves finding someone we like doing life with, we need Christ's help. In my marriage so far, I've learned a few necessary things that have helped me to live more "as one" with my spouse.

HUMILITY: Saying sorry is a huge thing. Being able to drop my pride and say I'm sorry has become a place of growth towards Christ every time it happens. Having the stance of "I'm perfect, I don't want to hear what you have to say" or trying to selfishly one-up my spouse makes it difficult to enjoy or want to be around each other. And it only makes arguments last longer. Humility gives God an opening where He can work.

COMMUNICATION: Speak! It took a year of marriage for me to realize I'm bad at reading minds. In fact, no one can read minds. If I'm feeling a certain way, I need to let my mate know in a way that is helpful, not harmful to our relationship. This includes communicating about plans. In Marriage, the two now become one. Our decisions affect the other person. Saying "yes" to one thing means we are indirectly saying no to something our spouse potentially wanted to do. Loving communication is the antidote to assumption.

ACCOUNTABILITY: I think accountability is necessary—even before marriage. Finding an older couple to help you spot pitfalls and land mines will only help you to have a stronger bond. When you experience difficulties, they can be a third party to help you understand what went wrong, and where you need to seek God. They can give you life examples from their own marriage of where they struggled and what they did to work on it. There is wisdom with age. Having couples in the same phase of life as you are is also beneficial. Knowing you're not alone in your struggles can be great encouragement and you can hold each other accountable and pray for one another.

PRAYER: Prayer is a necessity. God loves when we talk to Him. He loves when we go to Him for help even more. Marriage is hard. It's bringing two people with all their flaws together and saying, "go be perfect together." In the weakness of our marriage Christ wants to display His strength and power. Praying together aligns our hearts under His transforming power. It also knits us closer to one another.

Think about the "one-ness" level in your marriage. What is one change you can make in your own actions or thoughts to love your spouse better? Commit it to God, and with His help, begin doing it today.

Robert Kapen loves sports and was very active growing up in sunny Southern California. He loves writing and sharing life lessons, in hopes people can learn from them. He is going back to school to get a BA in English/Creative Writing. He wants to inspire people with his words of overcoming hardships and healing himself with writing as a form of therapy using the traumatic event God helped him through. In his recovery, he met a girl from Perú, and they live happily married for 8 years in the house he grew up in.

kapenwrites.com

WHAT WILL I SACRIFICE TO GET MY WAY?

JACQUELINE POPE

> *"Do nothing out of selfish ambition or vain*
> *conceit. Rather, in humility value others above*
> *yourselves, not looking to your own interests but each*
> *of you to the interests of the others."*

— PHILIPPIANS 2:3-4 (NIV)

"*L*et's just go our separate ways."

These are words that are often prematurely spoken in marriages today, and I've been guilty of speaking those very words in my own marriage. Few want to yield to the needs of each other. Often, it's all about "me" and what "I" want and what "I" need. Very little effort is put into growing or strengthening a marriage in unselfishness, and many are dissolved soon after getting started. Why? We live in a world of self-seekers. The oneness that was spoken in our vows have turned to "me-ness."

I say this not to point the finger at others but being reminded of my own selfishness within. I had the honor to have my husband bring to light what I had sincerely overlooked. There was something that I wanted to do, and I was adamant about it. I had "my" justifiable reasons for it and was standing my ground. It wasn't until my husband showed me that if I proceeded with what I wanted to do, it would have greatly affected the family financially.

I was blinded by my own selfish ambition and sincerely wrong. We have been sucked into TV, magazine and social media marriages that are a decorated farce. The phrase, "Happy wife, happy life" is lopsided. It may be comical on the surface, but it doesn't produce a joyful marriage for both spouses. Rick Warren said, "Babies by nature are completely selfish. They think only of themselves and their own needs. They are incapable of giving; they can only receive. That is immature thinking. Unfortunately, many people never grow beyond that kind of thinking."

For my marriage to be selfless, I need to focus on my spouse's needs—keeping in mind there are some things that only God can fulfill. We are instructed not to look to our own interests but on the interests of others. Through this, we will see stronger, fortified marriages which represent true love for one another and the love of God.

Heavenly father, I present my marriage to you and any selfish ways that are a part of me. You have been an excellent example of selflessness. Oh! that I may follow you and be considerate of the needs of my spouse and I pray they will do the same for me. In Jesus Name.

Jacqueline Pope is a wife and mother who enjoys mentoring and teaching others the Word of God. She is the author of Broken Hearts Forgotten Promises: Break the Cycle & Start Anew. Jacqueline is also founder of Refresh My Heart, a community that leads women's hearts to healing and transformation. She is passionate about encouraging others to walk in their call and make the most of every opportunity to be a light in a dark and dying world.   A few of her greatest joys are spending time with her husband, Regi and family and relaxing with a hot cup of tea.

amzn.to/3I6c3Ip

LEAD YOUR MARRIAGE

KRISTIAN KELLY

"Husbands, love your wives, just as Christ loved the church and gave himself up for her."

— EPHESIANS 5:25 (NIV)

For the first twelve years of my marriage, I let my wife lead. And by "let" I mean, I was too cowardly to step into any leadership position. The responsibility was one I wanted to hide from, but more than that, I was being petty. My mindset was, "I'll love her WHEN she shows me love and respect first." If it sounds childish, immature, and not Christ-like... that's because it wasn't.

As it turns out, I wasn't making it very easy for her to respect me. I did not realize that part of being my wife's "head" meant that I go first, because that's what Jesus did.

When I was blaming her and waiting for her to respect and love me more, I was actually placing the burden of headship (leadership) on her. It wasn't until I learned how to love and lead like Jesus that she began to respond beautifully.

In Ephesians 5:25, there is no caveat to loving my wife. "Love your wives," period. There is no waiting for her to do anything. Society tells us to only love when you are loved, as I stupidly agreed then. They also tell us men that we are bumbling idiots, unworthy of respect. Little did I know, I was perfectly portraying that characteristic. Regardless, we are to love as Jesus first loved us. Jesus came to us and loved us in order for our relationship with Him to be restored.

What does that look like? Look around your marriage and family. Then ask yourself, what's best? What's next? And take action. Do not be afraid, especially of her. She will respond. It will take time for her to see that her man is finally rising to the occasion. So don't falter when the first failure, disagreement, or disrespect occurs. Stand strong and learn. Love her like Jesus loves her. Show her His love through you. When this becomes who you are, you will see the love and respect.

God, I pray you help me be the man You designed me to be. Guide me into a stronger relationship with You. Give me the courage, wisdom, and compassion to be the leader for my wife and family that You blessed me with. Allow me to provide, cover, and protect my greatest blessings. Give me the desire to be the best man for them, and love them without selfish expectations. Help me love them just as You love me. Amen

Kristian is a warrior for Jesus Christ. He loves to draw people closer to God and their purpose in life. He is currently in his 14th year of marriage with his wife, Cristina and blessed with their son, Caedan. Kristian has been seeking God's plan for his life and believes he has found the mission he was created to fulfill; teach men to become Godly-masculine men who lead their family to strong relationships with Jesus. He prays the words God gives him will encourage and bless those who read them. To God be the glory. Amen.

COVENANTAL MARRIAGE VS. MARRIAGE CONTRACT

SHERRI HOWARD

"Our death is the only way we will ever be separated again."

— WEDDING VOWS

When people enter into any kind of contract, it is for each party's protection. They are in agreement that if one party does something to violate the contract, it is considered broken. At that point, the whole contract becomes null and void. So basically, each party agrees to hold up their ends of the contract as long as the other party holds up theirs too.

A covenant is different in that both parties intend to keep their agreement, even if the other party fails to keep their part of the agreement. If one party violates the covenant and fails to hold up their end, the other party is responsible to continue to do what they agreed to do. The covenant is not for either party's protection because in a Covenantal agreement they know that God is their ultimate protection.

Marriage is a Covenantal agreement, it is not a contract. A covenant is between three beings: a man, a woman, and God, who has joined them irreversibly together. The agreement of the covenant marriage is that we will be together, no matter what, "until death do us part." A covenant is a union that is totally focused on a personal relationship between two people who hold God at the center of all they do. Their purpose is to serve God and each other because they know when God wins, or their spouse wins, they win. It's a relationship that keeps no record of wrongs because they know no one is perfect and they cannot always serve each other perfectly. But because of the work of the cross and the Truth that Jesus has covered all of our sins, failures are forgiven. The more we understand the depths of our own failures, the easier it is to forgive the failures of others.

This is in stark contrast to viewing marriage as a contract. Instead of being a personal relationship, a contract is a professional relationship between only two people. Instead of the agreement lasting until death, it will last "until you do something that I don't like." It's an agreement where each party is seeking their own will and desiring to be served by the relationship. Each party keeps track of what the other party does/doesn't do, they record every failure in order to use it against their partner in order to get their own way. When one party fails to live up to expectations they deserve to be "punished" in one way or the other. The happiness of one party often takes away the happiness of the other, creating a win-lose scenario for the relationship.

When a couple enters marriage with a contractual agreement in mind, it leads to the idea of prenuptial agreements and "no fault" divorces. They actually enter the marriage with the thought that it is probably going to end. In far too many cases that kind of thinking leads couples into the self-fulfilling prophecy of divorce. Once we move marriage from a covenant to a contract, it becomes just a "legal thing" and it is no longer seen as a lifetime commitment before God.

Our modern day wedding ceremonies still follow the symbolisms of ancient Biblical covenant ceremonies. These ceremonies included the splitting an animal in two and passing down the "isle" between the two parts. In essence, a covenant was considered a very serious proposition where each party is saying, "Let this happen to us if we break this covenant." It was not permission for the other party to "cut them in half," it's permission for God to deal with them as they deserve. It was how they showed that they took loyalty seriously, deadly seriously.

In our wedding ceremonies, we don't cut an animal in half, but we do typically split the room in half with "her" side and "his" side. It is not only a symbolic gesture of two people joining and becoming one, it's also symbolic of the oath of the covenant. By passing through the middle of the two sides, each party is saying, "You are witnesses that God will deal with us justly if we break our covenant, because our death is the only way we will ever be separated again."

Lord, help me to remember my covenant vows. Give me strength and wisdom to apply the things of this book to my life and marriage. Help this knowledge be a weapon for my marriage and for those needing help with theirs. Amen.

Sherri Howard lives in Nesbit, MS with her husband Randy. They have three daughters and two grand daughters. Growing up she loved science but didn't care for English until a high school teacher sparked a love for writing. Her passion for writing has grown in conjunction with her love for God and He is by far her favorite subject. Sherri has spent time as a science teacher, a wife, a stay at home mom, an athletic director and as staff at her church. She has written many devotions for school and church news letters. At this time, she is a caregiver for her mom and grand babies, but continues to write when time permits.

MORE TOGETHER

CAROLYN DECK

"Also, one can be overpowered, but two together can put up resistance. A three-ply cord doesn't easily snap."

— ECCLESIASTES 4:12 (CEB)

'Created' appears three times in Genesis 1:27-28. God created men and women in His own image. He is loving, gentle, patient, kind, and full of grace and mercy. Then, He said "a man shall leave his father and his mother and hold fast to his wife, and they shall become one flesh."

Notice what followed: marriage. God designed this union to be good. He knew we needed each other.

God has richly blessed me with thirty-two years of marriage and five amazing children. God has given instruction, direction, correction, and protection throughout this time. He is so faithful. Through good times and bad, there have been many challenges; through sickness and health, God has been there. He *is* the third cord in our marriage.

Marriage always starts with love, but if left unnourished and uncherished, it will wither like the grass, fade, and fall like the flowers of the field.

So how does love grow? I believe humility is the glue that binds us together. I love how Rick Warren says, "it is not thinking less of yourself but about yourself less."

The game-changer for me was listening to the wife of a former World Vision Leader clarifying Eve as Adam's helper; *'ezer-kenegdo'*. This Hebrew word is frequently used to describe God; the one who does for us what we cannot do for ourselves—the one who meets our needs—He being our vital and all-powerful helper. Wow. How wonderfully fitting that 'ezer-kenegdo' is the word used to describe Eve. She certainly is not the lesser in the union. Marriage is not 50/50 but 100/100.

Heavenly Father, thank You for Your grace and abundance in my life that has enabled me to live as 'helper' in my marriage. I know even those overlooked and undervalued jobs I do daily matter. The tasks that have gone unnoticed by others, You sees. You know my moves and my motives— it all matters.

AS THE CHURCH

CAROLYN DECK

*"Conduct yourselves with all humility, gentleness, and
patience. Accept each other with love, and make an
effort to preserve the unity of the Spirit with the peace
that ties you together."*

— EPHESIANS 4:2-3 (CEB)

et's look at scripture again. Adam had a role to
play in this exchange, but sadly he failed his first
test. He did not stand up for his wife when the
serpent entered the garden. He was present but did not
speak out against the serpent. Adam should have stepped
in and repeated God's command to them not to eat of that
one tree. Instead, when God challenged Adam why they
were hiding, he started the blame game:

"It was the woman You gave me."

Wow, he blamed the woman AND God. Do you do
this when things don't work out? Note their cover-up: they
hid. Is this not true of sin? We don't like to be exposed;
the responses are blame, lies, and bad choices.

Ephesians 5 gives husbands explicit instructions: love your wives, just as Christ loved the church. That is a big deal. Christ loved us, His church, so much that He died for us. Christ's love is marked by giving not getting. His love makes the church whole. Christ's words for the church evoke beauty. Everything He does and says is designed to bring out the best in her. Furthermore, husbands are to love their wives as themselves: pampering, cherishing and nourishing.

Adam's disobedience brought about blame and shame, lies and loathing. These consequences resulted in the laboring we experience today. As God said it would be, so it is. God gave us a choice. Do you believe the lies and deceit of the devil or the truths of God?

This week, let's be intentional with our behavior. Let's aim to conduct ourselves with humility, gentleness, and patience. And to accept each other with love. Keep the peace, be fast to forgive, and be the first to say you're sorry.

Be strong in Christ's love and accomplish much together.

Heavenly Father. Thank you for being such a personal God. You knew it wasn't good for us to walk this life alone. Thank you for creating marriage between a man and a woman. Help us this week to open our eyes to Your goodness and provision, to be grateful, to see where we need to be humble, to say sorry, and to lift our partners up in Your love, cherishing each other as You cherish us. This we pray in Jesus Name. Amen

---

MY HUSBAND IS MY MINISTRY

MATEJA STOLNIK VUGREK

"Be devoted to one another in love. Honor one another above yourselves."

— ROMANS 12:10 (ESV)

I once heard from my spiritual mentor that my husband is my ministry. I thought, *"Hmm, yeah, I am serving my God, and I am in ministry. Why should my husband be part of it? It's too much."* When you look closer, you can see this has a deeper meaning.

Our God and His Son are perfect examples. Jesus was a servant with all his heart. Most of all, he wanted to serve his Father and people. They had a special covenant relationship. Moreover, they were always faithful to each other no matter what.

I like to see a covenant as a promise you cannot break. At weddings, many people read vows, promising each other faithfulness. That promise and those vows have a deeper meaning. We are entering into a covenant with each other. They should not be just empty words. They mean everything till we die.

Unfortunately, I was disappointed that some people in my life were not faithful, and they broke that covenant. But God grew me close to a few families so I could learn from them about true love and faithfulness. The kind we read from the Bible (Abraham and Sarah, Boaz and Ruth, Priscilla and Aquila and many more).

I had the honor to have one special couple that impacted me personally and in regards to my marriage. I was very encouraged until one day I found out that some of my favorite relatives and one person from my family were not faithful. I never thought that I would need to go through this. I was so disappointed, but as I was searching for answers, I saw that none of them were devoted Christians and they never had a godly example.

Still, I felt I should be comforted by God. And of course, He saw my cry, showed up, and reminded me that even when people are not faithful, He always stays faithful.

Dear ladies and sisters, even though some of your friends or even close family are not examples to you, please ask God for help. He will send you examples and encouragement. Only He knows what you need.

Even if you have not thought about that before or may not have the strength or hope for your marriage, He is willing to come and help you. How? He is a perfect giver. God's word says:

> "Now to him who is able to do immeasurably more
> than all we ask or imagine, according to his
> power that is at work within us."

> — EPHESIANS 3:20 (NIV)

We have and serve a God through whom nothing is impossible. Precious sisters, your dreams about godly marriage are not impossible to Him. He can give you fresh strength and love for your husband. He can work on your hearts and renew your love. Remember, both of you need to work and must be willing to stay in that covenant.

As Jesus was devoted to his Father, be devoted to each other. When he sees how you are devoted to Him first and then to each other, He will put His shield around you and your marriage. Who would refuse that?

God, I am so thankful for my marriage and ministry to my husband. Thank You that You have chosen him for me. Help me to be closer to You, so I can know Your heart at the deepest level. Please take all my selfish desires, sinful thoughts, and anything that can potentially separate me from my husband. Father, I ask that I will have each day new strength, patience, and love for my husband. Keep away everything that can separate us from You and one another. Give us the desire to honor You with our minds, hearts, desires, and bodies so we can be an example to others!

CHANGING THE APPROACH

JESSICA GRISSOM

> *"So in Christ Jesus you are all children of God through faith, for all of you who were baptized into Christ have clothed yourselves with Christ. There is neither Jew nor Gentile, **neither** slave nor free, nor is there **male** and **female**, for you are all one in Christ Jesus. If you belong to Christ, then you are Abraham's seed, and heirs according to the promise."*
>
> — GALATIANS 3:26-29 (NIV)

Several years ago, a time of crisis hit, and I was left feeling unraveled. I went through the stages of grief but got stuck in level 4—the state of depression. I didn't realize I was even stuck there until my husband and I had tough conversations and the subject would resurface. I realized I hadn't healed, and part of the reason was because I'd not taken the time to take practical steps to reconcile, define boundaries, state core values, and heal. As I started unpacking the whys, I realized that part of the problem was due to my theological beliefs. Although I said

I believed in an egalitarian approach, I was still holding onto complementarianism in many practices. These practices came from my subconscious, and I realized I had to further unpack the ideas and definitions before I could possibly move forward. I recognized that I was doing this difficult work because I loved Jesus and I wanted a godly marriage, but things were not working the way I'd learned.

My nature is more of a follower than a leader. I am a detailed person while my husband is more visionary. Even though I would say we were equals, I realized I was not directly communicating my needs, and this came from years of being raised in a fundamental church where women did not have a voice. One can look back in hindsight at situations and choose to stay in guilt saying, "I wish I would have handled such and such differently," but I decided that looking back with regretful thinking wasn't going to help rebuild our relationship. Unfortunately, the evangelical books I'd read on marriage regarding the issue were causing me to feel stuck. I was getting more upset and angrier because in reading the tips I felt like my needs were being silenced or, at best, minimized. In doing a lot of internal work, I decided to go to a licensed counselor and diversify the books I was reading.

Through all of it, I desired to have God at the center of my life and in our marriage. I went through a crisis of faith, not doubting if God was there or loves me but wondering how I was to handle one of my most important relationships. How was I to love and to love well? My husband and I talked, and we adapted some new practices in our relationship. It has been a journey, but my husband and I are together and working through things in a better way. We have learned a lot and continue to recognize things we need to work through. The journey is not easy, but we are still trekking forward and remembering this verse that has helped us confidently work together.

Dear Jesus, please help couples as they work through the challenges of life. Please help us realize where we are interpreting things that can become harmful to our relationships. Give us grace as we learn and help us understand that You want us to love each other deeply. Sometimes love means changing an approach, but it doesn't mean that we throw everything away. Help us use discernment as we grow in love. Help us keep You at the center of our lives. Amen.

KEEP DATING AND DREAMING

ANGIE WALTHALL

"For we do not wrestle against flesh and blood, but against the rulers, against the authorities, against the cosmic powers over this present darkness, against the spiritual forces of evil in the heavenly places."

— EPHESIANS 6:12 (ESV)

*M*arriage even at its best is hard. There's no other way to put it. As a picture of Christ and the church, Satan is constantly trying to tear apart and discount the validity of anything that might draw anyone closer to the LORD.

First of all, remember that you have an enemy, and it is not your spouse. Satan will do his dead level best to convince you that your spouse is your enemy. His goal is to divide and conquer. "The thief comes only to steal and kill and destroy. I [Jesus] came that they may have life and have it abundantly." (John 10:10 ESV).

Unite against the enemy, not each other.

This nugget is not just for the married. When we enter a relationship with Christ, our sin nature doesn't magically disappear. As we grow in maturity and deeper levels of sanctification, it gets easier, but we're not home free until we get HOME. So, find a group of true, trustworthy accountability partners and meet weekly—iron sharpening iron, in love asking the hard questions. It's easier to stay on track when you know someone who cares about you is going to ask those hard questions, and you have them to call or text for prayer when you're struggling.

Remember God's ways and thoughts are higher than ours. We won't always understand the trials we walk through, but we know that He will work them out for our good and HIS Glory. (Romans 8:28)

Find a good Biblical counselor you can talk to together and separately when issues arise. Proverbs (15, 20, etc) is full of wisdom regarding good counsel. Issues will arise where you will need help navigating. A mature, Biblical counselor will be able to walk you through scripture relating to issues you are facing. That will be invaluable to fight off the temptation to agree with the enemy that it would just be better to part ways. If you haven't done so yet, make up your mind together and individually to remove divorce as an option. Until death do us part, means just that.

- ***Keep dating FOREVER***—Cultivate an atmosphere of romance. The best way to do that is find out your spouse's love language(s). And let me assure you, they will not be the same as yours. Learn to speak their language; it's hard—like learning Greek, but it's necessary.
- ***Pray together***—There's nothing like hearing your spouse pray heartfelt prayers for you.

- **Dream together**—The LORD drew you together for a reason. Walk out the dream together that the LORD has placed in your hearts, and therefore fulfill HIS purpose in you. "For it is God who works in you, both to will and to work for his good pleasure." (Philippians 2:13 ESV)

Lord, I know that marriage is hard, but You've shown me that it is so worth fighting for. Thank you for all You've done for my marriage and my life, and everything that has brought me here. Amen.

PART II
OTHER FAITHFUL SPOUSES

We asked friends of Devo Writers (from the mailing list and social media) for marriage advice from a Christian perspective. This section is a collection of their answers. These contributors do not claim to be writers. However, most are in long-lasting marriages. As always, hold their advice up to *the* Word of God, and ask the Holy Spirit for guidance.

MARRIAGE ADVICE BITS

STANDOUT ADVICE:

"*I*n a gospel-centered marriage, you give yourself to your spouse regardless of the goods or the services because that's what true love is and because that's what glorifies God."
    -Matt Chandler, The Mingling of Souls

"Be more present, put the phone down, be more aware....Say, 'I'm sorry.' Better yet, say 'I was wrong,' and mean it...I'm signing up for being refined and it's gonna hurt—it's not natural...What we push back on most is usually what we need to work on most."
    -paraphrases from Worship Circle podcast "On Our Worst Day"

"As Julie and I celebrate 20 years of marriage today, here are 20 tips for a great marriage:

1. Learn your spouse's love language. (Julie's is acts of service, so doing the dishes means a lot more than flowers.)
2. Apologize even when you don't feel like it. Forgive even when your spouse doesn't apologize.
3. Pray with your spouse everyday. Yes, this one is hard to start, but once you do, it is so powerful.
4. Always have something planned to look forward to. Date night, weekend trip, concert, etc.
5. Love your spouse's family. They are now your family. (And they are awesome if you really get to know them.)
6. You can't change your spouse. But you can change yourself. Good habits begin with you.
7. Get the order right: God, spouse, kids. If the kids are the center of your life, it's time to reprioritize.
8. Decide to be married for life. No talk of divorce. No fantasizing about another spouse or an old dating partner.
9. Secrets will destroy your intimacy. It is better to be open and grow together than hold onto a secret and create a wedge.
10. Verbally compliment your spouse in front of your friends, kids, and in-laws.
11. Never give your spouse a reason to be jealous. Period.
12. Always call to say good night. (Even when you're traveling.)

13. Learn to love what your spouse loves. Watch the sports game. Say yes to the workout. Read the book.
14. Choose a solid, Bible-believing church and go all in. You'll need the community more than you know.
15. Ask your in-laws for advice. They are very wise.
16. Get hot. Get fit. Take care of yourself. You are the only permissible object of your spouse's sexual desire. Act like it.
17. Support your spouse's dreams. Yes, even the crazy ones. Don't shoot down their hopes. Find ways to support them.
18. Find a way to make their day. Leave a note. Fill up the gas. Make the coffee. Never stop dating.
19. Hire a bookkeeper and have a weekly financial meeting. Set money goals and celebrate small steps.
20. Love the Lord your God with all your heart, soul, and mind and love your spouse as much as you love yourself."

-Brian Dixon

"The truth is, without God in your life and marriage you cannot love at the depth of love that God wants to love you. Agape love as we find in the Bible is the most intense, everlasting, and uninhibited expression we can choose to share with one another. This is the way Jesus loves us."
-7 Truths of Marriage Devo from YouVersion

"One of the greatest lies the devil uses to discourage followers of Jesus is that (insert name here) will never change...if you have fallen into the belief that he or she will never change, then it's time for you to be the one who changes...No one is too far gone. There is no human still alive who is outside the not-impossible reach of God's forgiving and transforming grace...Nothing is impossible for God. He has the power to change people so they will start living the life He desires for them."

 -*Lies We Believe* (YouVersion Devotional)

———

"As their mutual goal is God's glory, when things get tough or they can't see eye to eye on temporal or personal matters, they are able to put those things aside and focus on that greater goal. This ability to step outside of themselves and their relationship and view things from God's eternal perspective gives their relationship meaning beyond their mutual benefit and makes it easier for them to find inspiration, contentment, and joy in their marriage even when their flesh tells them to be lazy or selfish."

"The world says to give only as much as you get, but Jesus says to give everything, expecting nothing in return. Serve your wife. Sacrifice for her. Demonstrate Jesus' humility as you do so, not because she deserves it—she may not sometimes—but because you're loving her the way Jesus loves the Church glorifies God."

 -Rewired Men Devo, Becoming the Man She Needs

———

"Your marriage is under attack because the devil hates when we glorify God, which is what marriage is meant to do. He has given the best of Himself to us so that we experience all of Him when together...God reconciled mankind to Himself in Christ; that's how our marital differences are reconciled, in Christ. If He can reconcile humanity to holiness, He can reconcile any marriage (exceptions for abuse)."

-Week 3 of "We Are a Zoo," Compel Church, Patrick Conrad

"Why do we bring out the worst in each other? That's one thing marriage is *meant to do*.

In woodworking, there's a technique called popping the grain or *water-popping*. It's useful for making cutting boards or pieces that will get wet. If you don't pop the grain, then sand it out, the wood grain and fibers will come up the first time it's used...which isn't good. It doesn't look or feel good and can even be dangerous. So, this is a preemptive move to smooth out the wood so that it is beautiful and useful right away.

In marriage, we are popping the grain on each other, bringing up fibers that otherwise stay hidden until tested. Then, we can personally choose to sand those down or work on removing, smoothing, so that we are better for one another the next time we are tested."

-Michael Lacey

SUPPORTER ADVICE

*H*ere's a collection of advice we received via social media and our mailing list from Devo Writers supporters. To consume or contribute content, sign up at ChristWriters.com and join our list.

MAILING LIST:

"As I was abused and told I didn't matter, I did not choose correctly when someone wanted me. Hence, you are not your own, plus bought with a price (Jesus's blood). It would have helped value myself and body better.

However, I learned to ask God to love my husband through me with His love. Love is a choice we make, to always think and speak and act as Jesus would, no matter the other's behaviour. Love covers a multitude of sins. It allows for healing and change, when nothing else does. It blesses both the giver and the receiver."

-from a long-time supporter and reader

"Number one: Forgive without limit. Secondly, never stop being each other's best friends. Treat one another like friends who enjoy just hanging out together! Keep your sense of humor. It goes a long way. After almost fifty five years of marriage, still adoring each other, my husband John and I found out what it meant when we vowed, "Till death do us part." I'm so glad to know that God walked us all the way through those years—some happy, some not so much—and He did it so beautifully. God did a very good thing when He invented marriage."

"We must stay strong and persevere with God who will make a way."

   -Susan Perry (Read Susan's devo here)

"Quickly forgive. Love like you would want to be loved. Treat your honey like you'd want to be treated. Show respect. Laugh a lot. Don't be afraid to laugh at yourself. Be quick to encourage and compliment them. Pray together. Show affection. Thank them. Show love in different ways. Be teachable. For a few. Lol"

FROM FACEBOOK:

Yes, some are cynical (or maybe tongue-in-cheek), some are funny, and some are right on the money. Take them with a grain of salt! Some of these even sparked full devotional pieces which made it into the previous section.

Guard yourself with the opposite sex. No opposite sex in your vehicle or home, etc without spouse or another adult.

or private conversations (minus therapy). If you wouldn't say it to the opposite sex with your spouse present, don't say it in private.

Keep dating FOREVER.

No matter what love your spouse the way God does.

Marriage is a covenant, not a civil union contract. The ceremony is rooted in an ancient covenant ceremony, study that!

Psalms.

Matthew 7 and Galatians 6—remember the log in your own eye/speak with humility/gentleness when there's conflict or a need to restore. I still get it wrong but have learned to ask forgiveness instead of stay stubborn/sinful.

Ephesians 4:32, Be kind to one another, tenderhearted, forgiving one another, as God in Christ forgave you.

The sweet old lady that signed our marriage license said, "Be good to one another" and it's the best advice I've ever been given!

"To the unmarried and the widows I say that it is good for them to remain single, as I am."

Don't be unequally yoked.

Out-serve each other.

God, Spouse, Children, Everything else —in that order.

Don't just be the spiritual leader of the household. God designed marriage specifically. Be the submitted to God leader your family needs.

Get out of this marriage before you meet your maker too soon.

Don't do it!

How many times shall I forgive them Lord? Seven times? Jesus: Seventy times seven.

Listen, Learn, and above all Love. Look to Jesus.

Speaking for my ex the phrase "burn her she's a witch" comes to mind.

Patience, kindness, and love.

Roses are are red, unless they are yellow, you better think twice before you marry that fellow. For the girl in town, get out of sight, after the makeup runs off, it may give you a fright.

Love and respect!

Marriage is hard, and kids make it harder. It gives you the opportunity to be more holy but not always more happy.

Psalm 23:1-6, I've been married for 30 years to a very strong willed woman. I think that passage is fitting. LOL.

It's better to be married than right.

"The faithful love of the Lord never ends! His mercies never cease. Great is his faithfulness; his mercies begin afresh each morning." -Lamentations 3:22-23 NLT

Choose your spouse every day! Every day matters. One unresolved unkind day can turn into a week. A month. A year. Fight against that by starting each new day showing grace and mercy.

Trust God's timing and his plan for your life.

Put your spouse first!!

Find a group of true accountability partners and meet weekly. Iron sharpening iron, in love asking the hard questions.

Remember God's ways & thoughts are higher than ours. We won't always understand the trials we walk through, but He will work them out for our good and HIS Glory.

Remember we do not wrestle against flesh and blood. We only have one enemy, & it's NOT our spouse.

Unite against the enemy not each other.

Find a good Biblical counselor you can both talk to together or separate when issues arise.

Pray together.

Dream together.

His people shall become my people.

Set boundaries early on!

What do you value more, unity or justice?

Be devoted to your man but also be with a man that will cherish you. If you are a believer and you are with an unbeliever, (just because they say they believe in Jesus does not make them a believer, Satan knows Jesus is real too.) I mean unbeliever as in; they are selfish, unkind, neglect you, criticize and blame you for everything wrong in the relationship; and they don't really want to be with YOU. Let them go. God wants you to have peace.

Submission isn't silence. And it isn't a warm fuzzy feeling. It's an expression of love to your Lord and the person with your ring on their finger. Jesus going to the cross wasn't a warm fuzzy feeling, it was the greatest expression in love....so we should expect that to be in His likeness, it will be difficult. But, it is far more rewarding than we could ever imagine when we do it His way.

And In dating....if the person is already wanting you to submit to sin in some area, RUN:) If you're meant to end up together, the Lord will take care of it, but then your'e not sacrificing your obedience.

Identify your spouses love languages and make every effort to love them in the way that speaks to them. The song and dance of hurt feelings can go on for years when one attempts to love others in their own love language. The discomfort and vulnerability of loving someone in a way that speaks to them rather than what is comfortable and familiar to us is sacrificial, beautiful, and wholesome.

A marriage has to have God at the center or it will never function properly like God intended.

Pray and always wait for God's answer. Sometimes no answer IS the answer.

Your children belong to God. You mold them for a short time. Lead them while you can to Heaven's glorious Gates

My advice is..spouse first.. when asked out... is spouse invited?? Why not? Bow out... never allow yourself in a situation if opposite sex alone.. spouse should always be invited.

Continually choose to allow the tough things to sanctify you, to become more holy rather than chasing my own happiness. And as a husband, love your wife as Christ loves the church...that's probably the hardest one for me!

One thing I started doing over the last year or so is being in the same room with my wife at night before bed...I know, what a wild idea?!

The thing is, I'm a very driven and ambitious person, and I have multiple businesses and pursuits that can take an infinitive amount of time. I was often leaving the bed before she woke and getting back in after she went to sleep - whether working in my shop or another room.

I realized that I wasn't investing time into one of the things I truly valued most: my marriage. I worked out the tithe to be 16.8 hours a week, and I wasn't even giving that to her.

As newlyweds, we were inseparable. And it showed in our bond.

THE MARRIAGE COVENANT

ANITA MUSE

"A joyful, cheerful heart brings healing to both body and soul..."

— PROVERBS 17:22 (TPT)

When we can love and see from the spirit and not our soul, we are ahead of the game—not just in marriage, but in life.

God created and ordained marriage between a man and woman and He said it was good. Although this covenant between a husband and wife is important to God, we often treat it lightly. We view it as more of an agreement between two people than a covenant between two humans and God. If we could wrap our hearts around the meaning of the word "covenant," it would help us realize what marriage was really meant to be: a Triune life!

After spending my first few years of marriage arguing and demanding my own way, I felt tired and grew to hate being married. I saw it as a very annoying contract. Then one day the Lord and I had a good talk about me, not my husband. Once I began looking at myself in the mirror and prayed about what was there, God began changing my wants and desires. Marriage was no longer about fighting for my own way, but about seeking what was good for my husband and our marriage. The change had to begin with me.

My happiest moment came when I found the courage to let go of what I couldn't change and placed it at the feet of Jesus. Weights I never knew were there began dropping off of my shoulders, and freedom came.

Once I experienced this moment, I stopped tearing down my marriage and began building it up. My husband and I started to pray and speak about the kind of marriage we really wanted. We found that God honors us praying together as a couple, for that is where the real power lies.

Because of finding the courage to let go of what I couldn't change and placing it at the feet of Jesus, I now have a completely new outlook on the marriage covenant I made before the Lord. My desire now is to be a good wife. I don't struggle with the silly things as much anymore, and my husband and I talk a lot more about our wants and our future together. I also pray for him as he daily strives to be a man of valor.

A joyful and cheerful heart in marriage only comes when we allow God to change our own hearts. Marriage isn't a simple verbal agreement. It isn't a business contract. It is a covenant that involves a triune relationship: God, myself, and my mate.

> *"For I know the plans I have for you", declares the Lord, plans to prosper you and not to harm you, plans to give you hope and a future."*

> — JEREMIAH 29:11 (TPT)

Lord, I ask your forgiveness for my arrogance in believing I can do marriage in my own strength. I can't. But You, Lord, desire to be at the center – changing my heart as You mold me into what You desire me to become. Thank You for Your faithfulness in healing my soul and in doing so, strengthening my marriage.

RUN WITH PURPOSE

JAMES POWELL

Autopilot is great for airplanes, but it's horrible for marriages.

*A*utomation has been something humans have attempted to implement in every aspect of life since the beginning of time. As technology advances, more and more tasks get automated. In 1903, the Wright brothers successfully created and flew the first manned aircraft accomplishing something that man had dreamed of for centuries. Just nine years later, another man figured out how to make the plane fly itself... sort of.

The goal should always be to automate the things that are less important in order to focus our attention on the things that are most important. Lawrence Sperry's intention behind inventing the first iteration of autopilot, was to automate only some of the basic tasks so that pilots could add more controls in the cockpit that deserved their attention and increased the machine's functionality. Regardless of Sperry's initial vision, however, every single control was eventually automated to the point that planes today can practically fly themselves. Don't get me wrong, autopilot is great for airplanes, but it's horrible for marriages.

The goal should never be to automate everything so that we don't have to focus on anything. The harder something is, the more we naturally desire to automate it. Relationships are hard work, and marriages take an exorbitant amount of hard work. So, it should come as no surprise that many couples in counseling pinpoint seasons when the relationship was running on autopilot as the birthplace of serious marital issues. Often distracted by stressors, both were checked out and in survival mode, leaving the marriage to fly itself. Rather than a conscious decision, this is most often a slow descent into the unintentional complacency of relational automation.

In 1 Corinthians 9:24-27, Paul is speaking of the need for self-discipline and focus when it comes to our spiritual lives. He uses the illustration of athletes in a race or a wrestling match to point out that these athletes are determined to endure strict training to run the race or fight at their best mental and physical condition. In other words, they're focused on what's important. He ends this analogy by saying he doesn't run aimlessly in his spiritual race or shadow box in the spiritual battles of life. He has purpose—intention—in every step and with every swing. His message is pretty simple—run with purpose. In our spiritual lives, our relationship with our spouse should be second only to our relationship with God. The only way to give our marriages the proper priority in life is to be intentional—taking every step with purpose.

Automation replaces intention. I can schedule a recurring text message to be sent to my spouse once a week that says, "Thinking of you" with a kissy face emoji, but that is the antithesis of thinking of her. When we allow our deepest earthly relationship to slip into autopilot, we're sending the message that our spouse is not worth our attention, opening the door for all kinds of unintentional mistakes. Controls in a cockpit don't care if you're being intentional about interacting with them, but your spouse does.

If you want to automate things in your life, have at it. Just make sure you're intentionally automating the things that rob your spouse of your attention in order to stay focused on the prize. Do the hard work of conditioning and self-discipline that it takes to truly love and respect your spouse. Run. With. Purpose. You'll be glad you did.

Lord, search my heart and point out any areas of my relationship with You or my spouse where I have traded intention for automation. Teach me to be relationally intentional and show me ways to love and serve my spouse that glorify You and strengthen our marriage. Help me to run with purpose in every step, Father. In Jesus's name, Amen

IT'S SERIOUS BUSINESS!
(EQUALLY YOKED)

KIM HARRIS

"Do not be yoked together with unbelievers...what does a believer have in common with an unbeliever..."

— II CORINTHIANS 6:14A & 15B (NIV)

To be yoked together is to be in a binding relationship. The warning is that a Christian should not enter a compromising personal or professional arrangement with a non-Christian.

The yoke is often used in the Bible to express the symbolism of having two that are similar in capacity so that they can both work together. As applied to marriage, to be unequally yoked means the intended. Partners will be working against each other instead of supporting each other. The work is harder, the yoke heavy. The success and enjoyment of the marriage is at great risk.

A marriage where two walk separately is not a marriage like our peace-loving God intended.

God designed marriage around oneness, unity, and intimacy. Being unequally yoked produces the opposite:

division, struggle, and frustration. For believers in Christ, intimacy, as God intends, is impossible without spiritual unity.

A Christian world view is different from a non-Christian. A Christian pursuing God and a non-Christian pursuing the world are going in two different directions.

Children too are affected by this unequal yoking. The shaping of their world view and life experiences is confusing, to say the least, as they live with parents modeling opposing lifestyles and values.

I speak from my own personal experiences. Having been in a 24 year unequally yoked marriage and parenting 3 children, I would encourage those seeking God's best to not be unwise. Don't rationalize your own desires or lean into your own understanding but rather choose to submit to His loving counsel. He is not trying to keep any good thing from us—quite the contrary. His ways can spare us heartache as He protects us.

Lord, thank You for how Your word lights the path I should walk on! Help me to trust that Your instructions are best for me and come from Your desire for my good and Your glory.

EVERYTHING YOU NEED FOR MARRIAGE

MARSHALL MASSEY

"Love is patient, love is kind. It does not envy, it does not boast, it is not proud. It is not rude, it is not self-seeking, it is not easily angered, it keeps no record of wrongs. Love does not delight in evil but rejoices with the truth. It always protects, always trusts, always hopes, always perseveres."

— 1 CORINTHIANS 13:4-7 (NIV)

When it comes to marriage advice, I couldn't think of a better verse. Everything you could possibly need to help you in a marriage is right here. How many times in your marriage have you been impatient, unkind, rude, self-seeking, easily angered? How about that fight you just got in with your spouse and you decided to bring up the past? That didn't work out to well, did it? Everything I mention above is the exact opposite of what love is. Therefore, it's so important to become more like Christ. The more we become like Christ the better we can show this kind of love towards our spouse. Instead of being impatient, rude, angry, self-seeking, or unkind let's replace that with the love of Christ. Be the man or woman God has called you to be. A loving patient, kind, happy, selfless, polite, and forgiving spouse.

Talking about 1 Corinthians 13:4-7 makes me think of my own marriage. I wish I could count on one hand how many times I was rude, impatient, angry or self-seeking, but I can't. I could probably write a book about how I have been all those things at some point in my marriage.

My wife and I have been married for 6 years this year and together for 9. Over the years we have had our challenges. It hasn't always been easy. At the same time, it has been amazing. We've had plenty of fights or arguments when we both handled things poorly. We would always come back and talk about it and eventually forgive each other and then move on. There have been times when we will go into the hallway of our home and read our wedding vows to each other that we have hanging on the wall as a reminder of why we got married, the commitment we made and the love at the center of it all. Part of my wife's vows to me writes, "You're patient when patience is needed, kind when kindness is undeserving, and loving even when I'm unlovable." Oh, how I love my wife. She is so much more of 1 Corinthians 13:4-7 than I could ever be and that I will be forever grateful for. God has blessed me beyond my wildest dreams.

I'd like to leave you with a simple prayer by praying 1 Corinthians 13:4-7 over you. Before I do that always remember, in the heat of the moment be the loving spouse Christ has called you to be. Be 1 Corinthians 13:4-7.

*Heavenly Father, I come to you right now and I pray 1
Corinthians 13:4-7 over whoever is reading this. I ask you
Lord to show us how to be patient, kind, and loving. Give
us the strength to not get angry, envious, proud or boast.
Show us how to be the love that is talked about in 1
Corinthians 13:4-7. Its in Your precious name we pray,
amen.*

SEEK GOD FIRST

SUSAN J. PERRY

*"But seek first the kingdom of God and His righteousness,
and all these things shall be added to you."*

— MATTHEW 6:33 (NIV)

*E*verything is based on seeking God first. This is wisdom. Jesus is the foundation of everything good. We want a good marriage, right? So let's go there. The Lord God Almighty should be first in everything you say and do and this scripture in Matthew is so right-on. When I learned this scripture, truly my life and my priorities changed, and life in Jesus Christ is better than ever. God wants us to seek Him first in all things because He should be our 'all in all,' as Colossians 3:11 says.

Our marriage is to be birthed in Christ Jesus because He is the foundation of all we do: the Cornerstone, the Capstone, and the Rock we must build everything upon. If not, then your marriage may be built on sinking sand. Like building a house, you first need a solid foundation. (See Matthew 7:25-27)

The Word of God helps to get a good start. It is a good blueprint for marriage. Because there are storms in life, storms in marriage and bumps in the road, we need a good foundation.

Here in America, we generally see concrete poured either as a basement up north or as a slab down here in the southern states. So no matter where we're from or where we are, we need concrete—a hard adhesive to keep everything together—hard as a rock that will remain stable to weather any storms that come along in the years to come.

Everything about our God is good. We need Him to bond our marriage together with love of the Holy Spirit to carry us through successfully and love our spouse as ourselves.

We can only do this through the Holy Spirit who is our enabler to love all, especially our spouses and our children. God gives us a lot of grace for both. While seeking God first and His righteousness, He will add all these good things unto us (see Matthew 6:33). We cannot do it without Him. We must seek God and His excellent choices for our lives as we come before the throne of grace, boldly yet humbly.

Who else are we to please and take delight in but our wonderful Lord, Jesus Christ? He will direct you to the right spouse, one of His wisest choice for your life because remember He knows the beginning from the end. He knows who will be good for you to know Him better.

God, You are the "Alpha and Omega, the beginning and the end, the first and the last." Help us to trust our marriages to You implicitly.

PERSEVERANCE

SUSAN J. PERRY

"per·se·ver·ance: persistence in doing something despite
difficulty or delay in achieving success."

— OXFORD DICTIONARY

here is perseverance needed in anything you want to do well. What is the most famous scripture that many Christians admit they want to hear when they get to Heaven?

"His Lord said unto him, 'Well done, thou good and
faithful servant: thou hast been faithful over a few
things, I will make thee ruler over many things: enter
thou into the joy of thy lord.'"

— MATTHEW 25:21 (KJV)

This takes perseverance and pressing into the Lord. We have not arrived yet. There is so much yet to do as perfection lies ahead of us in the Lord Jesus Christ. We have to stay in Him and persevere alongside Him.

The man who does not give up when tests come is happy. After the test is over, he will receive the crown of life. God has promised this to those who love Him."

— JAMES 1:12 (NLV)

I was recently in a vision in our home church here in Edgewater, Florida while in prayer time for revival on Friday June 4, 2021. We had talked about climbing the Mountain of God as in Exodus 24 with Moses and the 70 elders. All of a sudden I saw this foot starting to climb the base of the mountain and I saw a person just tilt his shoe towards me so I could see the cleats in the shoe and that was the end of the vision. We all need special spiritual equipment to persevere and climb God's mountain and this was a mountain climbing shoe I was shown during this time. I shared the vision with the group of prayer warriors and I admitted that I was not sure of the meaning. All of a sudden a mighty woman of God, my friend Elsie, shouted out, *"Perseverance, that's what that shoe represents."* And it all made sense; we will all need perseverance, patience and strength to make this climb because the road is paved with stones and crags and problems as well as many promises strewn about as we go. We must have a made-up mind to persevere and do so in God's will for our lives. Marriage is just one of our trial runs here on earth as we are tested for the real thing coming in heaven as we become the Bride of Christ.

Prayer will pave the way wholeheartedly going to God with all your intentions, your hopes, and your dreams. Staying in your first love with Him will prepare you for a good marriage. An intimate relationship with God the Father, God the Son, and God the Holy Spirit will guide you into all truth. As we put our marriage before God we are able to persevere.

THE DREADED S-WORD

AUBREE CLARK

"Submission is an expression of love, not a warm fuzzy feeling."

— AUTHOR UNKNOWN

The greatest expression of love known to man was an act of submission. I think we can all imagine that Jesus probably wouldn't have had a warm fuzzy feeling when he was thinking about the cross. Instead, it was more of a desire to submit Himself to the Father out of a deep love. Loving others doesn't always feel good in the moment.

Wives, there will be many times when you're trying to show respect to your husband that you won't have a warm fuzzy feeling – and you may not even feel like you have any love for him at the moment, but it will still be an expression of love. Not to him, but to Jesus.

If we read Jesus' prayer in Luke 22:42 of, "Not my will, but yours, be done," we see His extreme, complete, and absolute submission—all while sweating drops of blood from the stress caused by the impending horror and pain of a crucifixion. What we see here gives us the ultimate example to learn from so we too can submit ourselves to the Father's will through the Spirit like the Son.

The term submission has been given a bad wrap in our culture. Although it's often equated with inferiority, that isn't the biblical view. The Trinity is perfect, loving, relational, equal. and also submissive. It's the model for our marriages. Submitting to one another in love (but not sin) is our way to reflect the nature of the Trinity. We are submitting to God-given authority and ultimately God's authority. Wives and husbands are equal and made in His image, but He gave the responsibility of leadership to the husband. God gave a distinct order from the moment he created Adam followed by Eve. Wives, we are called to a disposition of submissiveness. This isn't for the husbands to command us, because it's already the Lord's command as His will for our life. We are called to this regardless of any sense of whether he's worthy of it. It's for us wives to willingly and lovingly offer.

We can read plenty of stories in the Bible where wives submitted to their husbands even when those men were far from perfect or their behavior far from being worthy of respect. They did it out of reverence to God. We do it even when it's not easy, when it's not convenient or comfortable, when it hurts our ego, or even when it seems infuriating. You alone have the ability to make your husband a greater man than he could ever possibly be on his own. You can also be the one to beat him down and make him weak by not honoring his deepest need of being respected. We as women have a lot of power in this.

The attitude and atmosphere of our homes largely depends on how we see & treat our husbands. If he is regularly the butt of our jokes, made to look like an idiot, or always wrong, we will lose out on experiencing the best and strongest version of our spouse. We will also be missing out on the opportunity to display the transformative work of the gospel in our lives to others around us.

We are not perfect, and our spouse isn't either. This means we should be able to start each day saying to each other, "You're not perfect but you're trying, same as me." God's love isn't based on performance, so ours shouldn't be either. It's not about trusting your husband; it's about trusting God and His leading of him to lead you. It's an expression of love.

Thank You for giving me Your Word that so clearly shows submission through Your great love for us. Give me the courage to choose to submit my life to You daily, even in the difficult things. Let my life and marriage glorify You and be evident to those around me. Remind me to trust You at times I don't want to submit, and to be grateful that Your love for me is not based on my love for You.

KIDS COME THIRD

TERRAA GENTRY

Adding children to our family has been an enormous blessing. It has also been very straining on our marriage.

On more than one occasion, either myself or my spouse have put our kids' wants or desires before God's plans and our marriage's needs. The result has been hurt and resentment. I believe this hurt and resentment was a direct result of how far we stepped away from God's design for our marriage. God designed marriage to be a reflection of His love for us. Ephesians 5:25 (NIV) tells us "Husbands, love your wives. Love them, just as Christ loved the church. He gave himself up for her."

When we married, we became one (Genesis 2:24). My marriage to my spouse is a single unit that reflects how Christ loved the church. I've personally found that having a constant and unfailing relationship with the Lord can give us what we need to love our spouses. We activate our affections toward God by engaging in prayer and immersing ourselves in His living Word, which in turn shows us how to love our husbands or wives with action.

I believe the way our children learn to love themselves and others is affected by the way they see us loving the Lord and others. They learn about relationships and love by witnessing us prioritize God above everything else, and by the way we love our spouse in a Christ-like manner. God is number one, our spouse is number two, and the kids come third.

God, thank you for Your unending love. We thank You for the design of marriage to be a reflection of Your love. Help us to remain close to You through Scripture and to love our spouses as You have loved us. Father, we pray that our children would recognize what love looks like by the reflection of You in our marriage. May we point our children toward You in all things. In Jesus name, Amen.

BETTER TO BE RIGHT?

PATTI WENDEL

"It's better to be married than right."

— AUTHOR UNKNOWN

I grew up in the era of *Happy Days* and *Laverne & Shirley*. I loved those shows. I loved those characters. They made me laugh. I could relate to almost all of them in some way, but the one I understood the best was "The Fonz" – Arthur Herbert Fonzarelli. It wasn't for his love of the opposite sex, nor his perfectly coifed hair—although I'm all about a nice head of hair. What resonated with me about Fonzie was his absolute inability to say he was "wwww-wrrrr-wrooo-wron----." He couldn't even say the word.

Why was I like that?? Because being wrong (see I can at least say it) made me less. It made me less intelligent. It made me less informed. It made me less. And I was terrified of being less.

Unfortunately, I carried that feeling into my early (and maybe not so early) years of marriage. I had to be right. At all costs. Even when deep down I knew I was wrong, I couldn't let it show. I was still afraid of being less. Then I read Proverbs 21:9, which says,

> *"It's better to live alone in the corner of an attic* (some translations say "roof") *than with a quarrelsome wife in a lovely home."*

It struck me.

Even though I was working very hard to make a lovely home for my husband and I to dwell in, I was making my husband miserable – wishing he could go live on the roof all by himself. Why? Because I was afraid to be less. Once again, insecurity had taken over my life.

Brene' Brown says in her book, *Atlas of the Heart*, that the opposite of personal insecurity is *self-security*. Researchers define that as "the open and nonjudgmental acceptance of one's weaknesses." Accept my weakness? WHAT?? Can I do that?? But the bigger question was – am I willing to damage my marriage because I'm afraid to admit I have weaknesses and that I'm not always right? I had to make the call. Did I want to be right or did I want to be married?

Admitting that I was not always right, admitting my insecurity, and admitting my weakness opened me up to a more successful marriage of being emotionally close to my husband and eventually my children. They all knew something I was finally willing to admit: I didn't always have to be right – nor *was* I always right. Losing an argument used to infuriate me and cause me to feel defeated because it ate away at my security. But did it really?

When I finally started admitting that I was wrong– guess what? They didn't all leave me because they thought

I was stupid. Everyone is wrong at some point. The only perfect One is our Creator. When I stopped always having to be right, I became more emotionally healthy and became more likely to have emotionally healthy relationships.

My dearest Creator God – I admit that I have been wrong – a lot. But I thank You that You have placed people around me that love me with all my faults and insecurities. Thank You that Your word opened my eyes to how miserable I was and especially how miserable my spouse was – and I pray that You will do the same for anyone willing to admit that it's better to be married than right.

SPIRITUAL DUTIES OF A HUSBAND

DUKE IVY

"Husbands, love your wives, just as Christ loved the church and gave Himself up for her to make her holy, cleansing her by the washing with water through the word, and to present her to Himself as a radiant church, without stain or wrinkle or any other blemish, but holy and blameless."

— EPHESIANS 5:25-27 (NIV)

husband is to love his wife with the same selfless and sacrificial love that Christ has for His church. That's a powerful command, brothers. Christ gave everything He had, including His own life, for the sake of His church. Husbands, you're to display this same sacrificial love by devoting your time, energy, and resources to your wife and family. In the end, a husband who loves His wife, with this unselfish love, brings great blessings to himself from his wife and from the Lord.

Let us move on to verse 26 which says, "to make her holy (sanctify in the "KJV"), cleansing her by the washing with water through the Word." The husband is the spiritual leader of his family and it's his responsibility to read, study, know, teach, and speak the Word to his wife and family. It is his duty to wash his wife with God's Word by teaching her and leading her in His Word.

Verse 27 goes on to say, "and present her to Himself (God) as a radiant church, without stain or wrinkle or any other blemish, but holy and blameless. It's the husband's duty to "present his wife" to God as pure, holy, and blameless. This means he is responsible for her knowledge of God and His Word, and the purity of her walk with God. A Christian husband shouldn't be able to bear the thought of anything sinful in the life of his wife that is displeasing to God. His greatest desire for her should be for her to become perfectly conformed to Christ so he leads her to purity.

1 Peter 3:7 in the NIV says, "Husbands, in the same way be considerate as you live with your wives, and treat them with respect as the weaker partner and as heirs with you of the gracious gift of life, so that nothing will hinder your prayers."

It's the husband's loving duty to be considerate and sensitive to the needs, fears, desires, and feelings of his wife. While the wife is the physically weaker partner in need of her husband's protection, provision, and strength, she is, however, fully equal in Christ – spiritually and intellectually. A good wife is a divine blessing and favor from the Lord (Pro 18:23), and she must be treated as such.

Here's a point to ponder: the way you treat your wife matters so much in the eyes of God, that mistreating her can cause your prayers to be hindered! Now that's something to think about and meditate on.

SPIRITUAL DUTIES OF A WIFE

DUKE IVY

> *"Wives, submit yourselves to your own husbands as you do to the Lord. For the husband is the head of the wife as Christ is the head of the church, His body, of which He is the Savior. Now as the church submits to Christ, so also wives should submit to their husbands in everything."*

> — EPHESIANS 5:22-24 (NIV)

These scriptures teach us that a wife is to submit herself to her husband as she does to the Lord. This is a deep teaching that some may find hard to grasp because of the influence of our society today. However, we as believers aren't supposed to follow the ways of the world, but we're called to follow the Word of God.

The English word "submit" comes from the original Greek word "hupotasso" which means to place or put under. So it's the wife's duty to place or put herself under the authority of her husband as the head of their household. This submission is not the husband's to command but for the wife to willingly and lovingly offer. The wife's perspective should be that she faithfully and lovingly submits herself to her husband as an act of obedience to the Lord — which she can easily do if her husband is properly following God and His Word.

The husband's role in leading his family is God-ordained and the wife must recognize this as she follows him. As the husband leads his wife by the Word of God, and she submits to his leading, it will pour out so many of God's blessings upon their lives.

In Genesis 2:18 God says, "It is not good for the man to be alone. I will make a helper suitable for him."

God knew it wasn't good for man to be alone and made a "helper" so man would have a companion. The Hebrew word "ezer" was originally used as the word "helper" in this Scripture. But the English sense of the word is too weak to describe how important God's creation (the woman) truly is. As we look at the original Hebrew word "ezer" we see it carries a sense of strength and rescue.

Further study describes the wife "helper" as vitally important (like a doctor) and having powerful acts of rescue and support (military aid in battle). Wives, your role is to help your husband in this life and support him in any area he is lacking. You're to be his strength and come to his rescue as the battle rages on in your lives. When he or your children are sick or broken it's your duty to doctor them back to health. You're so special and vital to his life, without you his life would be incomplete.

———

Duke Ivy doesn't let his incarceration stop him. He writes as Preacher Joe from his cell and has recently released a book of devotionals:

I Am Found: Finding God's Light in the Darkness

MORE DEVO WRITERS COLLABORATIONS

Be sure to check out the growing series of Devo Writers Collaborations.

amzn.to/3HQuscb

Get the FREE Hope Garden Study Journal which can be used daily or weekly. It includes a worship section with links to worship songs. Get the print version or use the digital as a great journal accompaniment! Oh, and did I mention it's FREE?

LAST REQUEST

You probably got this book based on a positive online review or someone's glowing recommendation.

We believe in the power of reviews (and so do online bookstores), so in efforts to help as many people as possible by getting the book into more hands, we're asking something of you:

Go to you recent Amazon Orders, and please leave an honest review on Amazon!

It can be a simple sentence or several paragraphs, and you can submit one after simply reading one or two devos.

Thank you so much!

Made in the USA
Coppell, TX
02 March 2023